Gnosticism and Gnosis
An Introduction

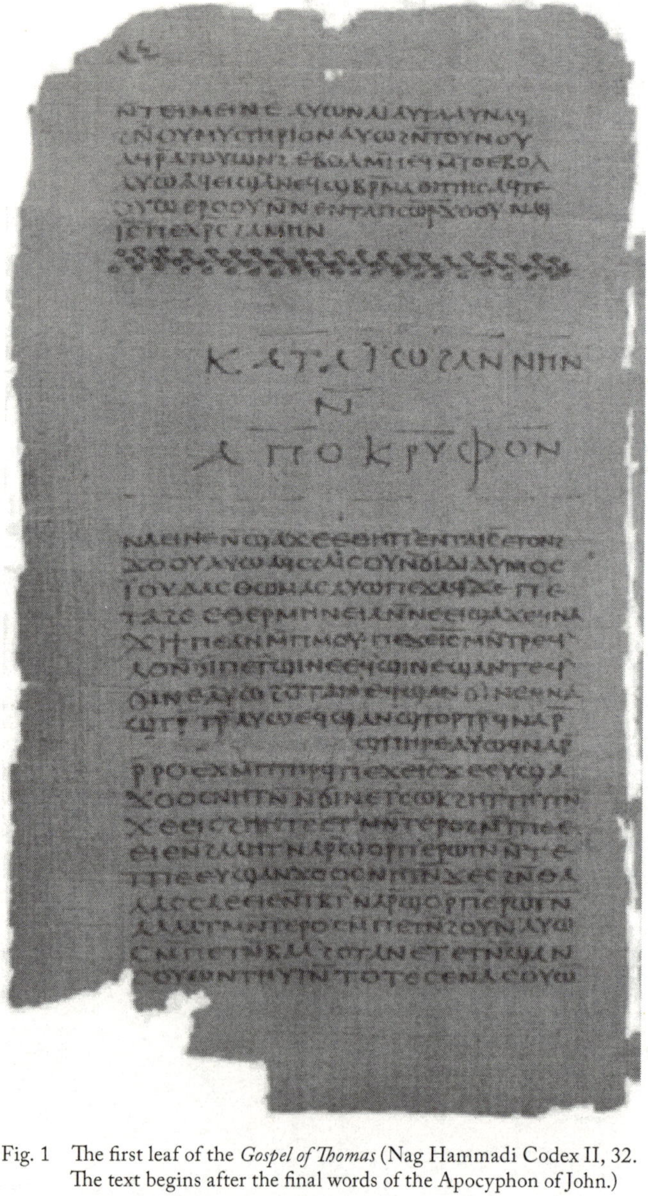

Fig. 1 The first leaf of the *Gospel of Thomas* (Nag Hammadi Codex II, 32. The text begins after the final words of the Apocryphon of John.)

Gnosticism and Gnosis

An Introduction

by

R.A. Gilbert

ANTIOCH PAPERS
BRISTOL 2012

First published
6th October 2012
by Antioch Papers
an imprint of
Imagier Publishing
Rookery Farm
Bristol, BS35 3SY
United Kingdom

E-mail: ip@imagier.com
www.imagier.com

Copyright © R.A. Gilbert 2012

The right of R.A. Gilbert to be identified as the author of this work has been asserted by him in accordance with the Copyright, Designs and Patents Act 1988

All rights reserved. No part of this publication may be reproduced, stored in or introduced into a retrieval system, or transmitted, in any form, or by any means, electronic, mechanical, photocopying, recording or otherwise, without the prior written permission of the publisher. Reviewers may quote brief passages.

ISBN 13: 978-0-9568789-8-4

Cover and text design by Allan Armstrong
The paper used in this publication is from a sustainable source and is elemental chlorine free.
Printed and bound by CPI Group (UK) Ltd, Croydon, CR0 4YY

Contents

Illustrations vi

Foreword 1

Prolegomena: What is Gnosticism? 5

The Origins of Gnosticism and the
        Sources of Our Knowledge 15

Gnostics and Their Teachers:
        Systems of Gnostic Belief 36

The Gnostic Diaspora:
        Gnosticism after Nag Hammadi 67

Clinging to the Wreckage:
        Gnosticism Today: Revived or Alive? 104

Further Reading 127

Index 132

Illustrations

Fig. 1. The first leaf of the *Gospel of Thomas* (Nag Hammadi Codex) . . . . frontis

Fig. 2. Diagram from *The Book of Jeu,* Chapter Seven (Bruce Codex) 4

Fig. 3. Hippolytus of Rome 20

Fig. 4. Nag Hammadi in Upper Egypt 68

Fig. 5. Mani 82

Fig. 6. Henry More 103

Foreword

As you take up this little book you may reasonably ask why, when there is already a vast literature relating to Gnosticism, it has been written, and why should I, a non-specialist, have written it? First, then, the question 'why?'

It is certainly true that there are many existing texts and translations of gnostic writings, and far more critical studies, commentaries and interpretations of them, but there is no ready guide for the novice as to the quality, usefulness, objectivity or availability of this literature. Thus anyone who has encountered the word 'Gnosticism', but who knows little of what it means, faces a significant problem when trying to find meaningful answers to the questions that arise.

The novice enquirer may, of course, turn to the Internet, but if the following brief terms (and they are only examples) 'books on Gnosticism' and 'gnostic texts' are entered into the largest Internet search engine, then he or she will be faced, respectively, with 152,000 and 384,000 entries. They are not easy to sift and many of them blandish the reader as seductively as the elfin pedlars in Christina Rossetti's poem 'Goblin Market' – and with the risk, metaphorically, of equally dire results.

There are introductory works on both 'Gnosticism' and 'gnosis', but they are mostly written for an academic readership and tend to be highly technical and to require a more than

Gnosticism and Gnosis: An Introduction

basic understanding of ancient religions and of Old and New Testament studies. Books for the general market are, inevitably, populist in tone and usually uncritical in their approach. They are, all too often, also lacking in objectivity – a lamentable failing that is not confined to popular books: a partisan viewpoint can creep, all too easily, into more scholarly works also.

In this brief, introductory survey I can offer no final conclusions and I have attempted simply to present a reasonably objective view of ancient Gnosticism and of the gnosis that it represents, setting out their nature and principal features, their probable origins, their significance and their history, together with a brief explanation of how our present knowledge of them came about. Beyond this I have given an outline of later dualist belief systems that have been – rightly or wrongly – labelled as 'gnostic', and I have tried also to address the issue of the contemporary understanding and relevance of Gnosticism: what it means for those who perceive themselves to be gnostics or, in some sense, seekers after gnosis. Inevitably, it has proven impossible to avoid a degree of subjectivity in arriving at my conclusions on this, although I trust that my personal beliefs and attitudes have not unduly coloured my judgements.

Which brings us to the author. What has led me to write this book? Although I have edited and introduced the works of distinguished scholars in this field, my own specialist area has been the history and interpretation of aspects of the Western Hermetic Tradition in the nineteenth and twentieth centuries. Such knowledge and understanding of Gnosticism and gnosis as I have has come as a result of my study of the roots of Western Hermeticism, while my fascination with the many puzzles and

Foreword

unanswered questions surrounding Gnosticism – some of them perhaps unanswerable – has been fuelled by a deep and abiding interest in the origins and nature of the Christian faith and a parallel fascination with dualist religions. It does not seem to me unreasonable that an educated and intelligent layman, who is also a believing and practising Christian, should make use of such knowledge and insight as he possesses in order to try to present an accurate, objective and serviceable introduction to a complex and controversial topic.

If I have succeeded in my aim I shall be satisfied, but any praise should be given to the many authors whose work I have utilised, and to whom I am greatly indebted. Such faults as this book possesses are mine alone.

Robert A. Gilbert
Tickenham, June 2012

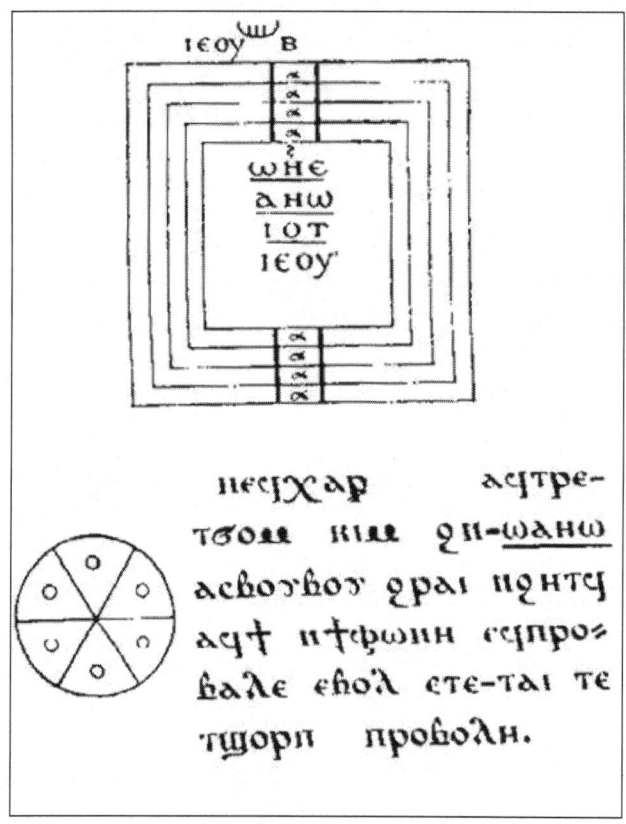

Fig. 2 Diagram from *The First Book of Jeu*, Chapter Seven (Bruce Codex)

Prolegomena: What is Gnosticism?

Gnosticism is an invented word for a faith – for want of a better noun – that bedevilled the early Christian Church with which it co-existed. Its various forms faded away in the declining Roman Empire and it was effectively ignored until the eighteenth century, when historians of Christianity took up serious study of the milieu in which the early Church had developed. Outside this limited circle of scholars knowledge of, and interest in, Gnosticism was minimal and remained so until the discovery of a gnostic library in 1945. As translations of the books it contained began to appear, public curiosity was piqued and a fascination with these extraordinary texts rapidly grew. Gnosticism, however much misrepresented and to whatever degree misunderstood, improbably became fashionable. Today it is also ubiquitous.

Gnostic ideas, or what are presumed to be such, have permeated religious philosophy and popular psychology and are equally at home in cinema and literature. Why this should be so is not immediately clear. There is certainly great popular appeal in the story of the remarkable discovery that brought Gnosticism out of its ancient backwater into the full light of day, and of the ensuing, and continuing, academic rancour that has followed. But that alone does not fully explain why

Gnosticism and Gnosis: An Introduction

the philosophy of this strange ancient faith, the concepts and doctrines of its many varieties, and its seeming practices, should have so seized the public mind that gnostic churches have been founded and embraced. Nor does it explain why eminent artists, writers and psychologists have identified themselves as 'gnostics' and espoused the spiritual knowledge – the 'gnosis' – that supposedly lies at the heart of this newly revived system of beliefs.

Here we may ask, 'Does it matter? Why should we concern ourselves that a long-dead religion has been brought back to life? These are legitimate questions, for Gnosticism is, and was in its own day, a minority pursuit; so is there any real need to seek an explanation for its revival? I believe that there is, for if we can discover just why and how this improbable revival has come about, and if we can understand just what it is in Gnosticism that fuels its contemporary appeal, then we can better understand the origin and nature of our spiritual impulses. I also believe that such a quest is necessary if we are to identify what needs to be done in order to restore accessible, appropriate and desirable forms of spirituality to demoralised and failing institutional Churches.

Arriving at conclusions to all of these issues will not be a sufficient step to attain this restoration, but it will be a significant and, I believe, a necessary one. But before we set out on this quest we must establish one thing above all: what exactly is Gnosticism? And here our difficulties begin.

What is Gnosticism?

The problem of definition

The term 'gnostics' (γνώστικοι) was first applied, with approval, in early Christian communities to Christians who sought for 'gnosis', or 'the knowledge of insight', which was perceived, in the words of Clement of Alexandria, as 'a kind of perfection of man as man, harmonious and consistent with itself and with the divine world, being completed, both as to the disposition and the manner of life and speech, by the science of divine things'. It had, Clement maintained, been 'handed down by tradition according to the grace of God',[1] and it is only those possessed of the true gnosis who deserve the name of 'gnostics', for, he wrote,

> the gnostic alone, having grown old in the study of the actual Scriptures, guards the orthodox doctrine of the Apostles and the Church and lives a life of perfect rectitude in accordance with the Gospel, being aided by the Lord to discover the proofs he is in search of both from the law and the prophets. For the life of the gnostic, as it seems to me, is nothing else than deeds and words agreeable to the tradition of the Lord.[2]

In this sense the gnostic and his gnosis were wholly orthodox: an inspired Christian, who had studied the Scriptures deeply and so gained a profound insight into the nature and relationship of God and man, in both this world and the next. But another meaning of these terms also gained currency as the somewhat

---

[1] *Miscellanies [Stromateis] Book VII.* X. Section 55. See the edition of the Greek text, with translation, by F.J.A. Hort and J.B. Mayor. London, 1902, p. 97.

[2] *idem.* XVI. Section 104. p. 183.

Gnosticism and Gnosis: An Introduction

fluid forms of the earliest Christian communities gradually coalesced into one dominant form, with the essential doctrinal features that would become, despite its multiplicity of warring denominations, the 'orthodox' Christian faith that has survived to the present day. This other form of gnosis was, in the view of the proto-orthodox, those 'opposing ideas of what is falsely called knowledge (γνωσις)', which St Paul warned Timothy to avoid because 'some have professed [it] and in so doing have wandered from the faith' (1 Tim. 6:20-21).

The various forms of this 'false' gnosis provided the foundations on which gnostic schools of thought built their systematic presentations of doctrine and practice, in opposition to the orthodox varieties of Christianity that were evolving and establishing themselves at the same time. But it was the vibrant orthodox faith that proved to hold the greater appeal to the spirit of the age, that eventually became the official religion of the Roman Empire, and that succeeded while the gnostic schools failed. Why this should have been so is still a debated issue – as is the question of the current enthusiasm for gnostic beliefs – but before we consider it we must establish our definition of Gnosticism and distinguish its doctrinal content from that of orthodox Christianity.

From the beginning, and even more so at the present day, definers of the term 'Gnosticism' have tended to follow the approach of Humpty Dumpty, who told Alice that, 'When I use a word ... it means exactly what I choose it to mean – neither more nor less'.[3] It also serves as one of his 'portmanteau' words,

---

3 [C.L. Dodgson], *Through the Looking-Glass and What Alice Found There*, by Lewis Carroll. Macmillan, 1872, p. 124.

What is Gnosticism?

for it is a notoriously imprecise term, a container for a large and shifting population of ideas, beliefs, attitudes and ways of being, varying according to the preconceptions and agendas of its many and various definers. The first to use the word was the English philosopher and theologian, Henry More, who in 1669 applied it in a pejorative sense to condemn Roman Catholicism as a heresy: 'it is', he wrote, 'the old gnosticism writ large'.[4] Thus the whole range of beliefs of the different schools of gnostics were gathered together and presented as one systematic heresy: one religion, separate and distinct from the Christian faith. And this has coloured, or rather bedevilled, subsequent perceptions of Gnosticism as students of early church history and doctrine have tried to squeeze all gnostics into a single, restricted category. It was never an easy fit, and since the middle of the twentieth century this restricted usage – of a distinct religion, defined by its dualist beliefs – has begun to fall apart.

The weakness of such restriction was recognised much earlier, by George Salmon,[5] one of the more careful of church historians and theologians of the late nineteenth century. He recognised that defining Gnosticism was 'a point on which writers are not agreed', and while he used the word in a rather narrow sense, he admitted that this was a debatable issue, 'Gnosticism not being a word which has in its own nature a definite meaning'. He added that, 'There is no difficulty in naming common characteristics of the sects commonly called

---

4 *An Exposition of the Seven Epistles to the Seven Churches together with a brief Discourse of Idolatry, with application to the Church of Rome.* London (1669).

5 The Revd George Salmon (1819-1904) was an Irish mathematician and theologian, who became Regius Professor of Divinity at Trinity College, Dublin.

Gnosticism and Gnosis: An Introduction

Gnostic, though perhaps none of them is distinctive enough to be made the basis of a logical definition'. [6] This led him to the cautious conclusion that,

> We come very close to a definition if we make the criterion of Gnosticism to be: the establishment of a dualism between spirit and matter; and, springing out of this, the doctrine that the world was created by some power different from the supreme God, yet we might not be able to establish that this characteristic belongs to every sect which we count as Gnostic. [7]

Other scholars tended to follow this point of view, often with less reservation, but changing views on the understanding of biblical texts, and the discovery of a gnostic 'library' in 1945, led to reappraisals of both Gnosticism and early Christianity. Gnosticism, especially, seemed to require radical reinterpretation and for specific boundaries to be set as to its meaning. Attempts to do this, however, have never been wholly successful – as even the more comprehensible parts of the following tortuous 'working hypothesis' of 1966 make clear:

> The Gnosticism of the Second Century sects involves a coherent series of characteristics that can be summarized in the idea of a divine spark in man, deriving from the divine realm, fallen into this world of fate, birth and death, and needing to be awakened by the divine counterpart of the self in order to be finally reintegrated...

6 George Salmon, 'Gnosticism', in W. Smith & H. Wace (Ed), *Dictionary of Christian Biography*, London, 1877–1887, Vol. 2, pp. 678-687. See p. 678.

7 *ibid.* p. 679.

What is Gnosticism?

> Not every *gnosis* is Gnosticism, but only that which involves in this perspective the idea of the divine consubstantiality of the spark that is in need of being awakened and reintegrated. This *gnosis* of Gnosticism involves the divine identity of the *knower* (the Gnostic), the known (the divine substance of one's transcendent self), and the *means by which one knows* (*gnosis* as an implicit divine faculty is to be awakened and actualized. This *gnosis* is a revelation-tradition of a different type from the Biblical and Islamic revelation-tradition).[8]

Subsequent definitions and descriptions of Gnosticism by scholars in this field have aimed at greater clarity and attempted to be more succinct, although none has been universally accepted. For example, Bart Ehrman describes Gnosticism as,

> A group of ancient religions, which were closely related to Christianity, that maintained that sparks of a divine being had become entrapped in the present world and could escape only by acquiring the appropriate secret gnosis ... of who they were and of how they could escape. This gnosis was generally thought to have been brought by an emissary descended from the divine realm.[9]

And for Harold Attridge, Gnosticism is,

> [A] generic term for a variety of religious movements of the first centuries of the Christian

---

8 Ugo Bianchi (Ed.), *The Origins of Gnosticism. Colloquium of Messina 13 – 18 April 1966.* Leiden, 1967, pp. xxvi-xxvii.

9 Bart D. Ehrman, *Lost Christianities: Christian Scriptures and the Battles over Authentication.* Chantilly, VA, 2002, p. 124.

Gnosticism and Gnosis: An Introduction

> era. Although the theology, ritual practice and ethics of these groups differed considerably, all purported to offer salvation from the oppressive bonds of material existence through gnōsis, or 'knowledge.' Such knowledge was diverse, although it regularly dealt with the intimate relationship of the self to the transcendent source of all being, and this knowledge was often conveyed by a revealer figure.[10]

Definitions such as these are, however, often criticised for being too limited. The two above both emphasise the association of Gnosticism with Christianity, a relationship disputed by others. Thus, Karen King states that Gnosticism 'has mistakenly come to be thought of as a distinctive Christian heresy or even as a religion in its own right, and libraries are replete with books describing its central beliefs, discussing its origins, and considering its history'. She also argues, in answering the question 'Why is it so hard to define Gnosticism?', that the problem lies in,

> a rhetorical term [having] been confused with a historical entity. There was and is no such thing as Gnosticism, if we mean by that some kind of ancient religious entity with a single origin and a distinct set of characteristics. Gnosticism is, rather, a term invented in the early modern period to aid in defining the boundaries of normative Christianity.[11]

---

10   Harold W. Attridge, 'Gnosticism', in Paul J. Achtemeier (Ed.), *Harper's Bible Dictionary*. San Francisco, 1985, p. 349.

11   Karen L. King, *What is Gnosticism?* Cambridge, MA, 2003, pp. 1-2.

What is Gnosticism?

King is not alone in rejecting narrow boundaries for Gnosticism. Michael Williams, in his original and highly influential study, *Rethinking 'Gnosticism'* (1996), states that,

> What is today usually called ancient 'gnosticism' includes a variegated assortment of religious movements that are attested in the Roman Empire at least as early as the second century C.E. ... The term 'gnosticism' in modern discourse has become such a protean label that it has all but lost any reliably identifiable meaning for the larger reading public.[12]

Karl Luckert goes even further in arguing for the effective meaningless of 'Gnosticism' as a label:

> Defining gnosticism or gnosis, humanly speaking, is an impossibility. It may be said that the task of studying gnosticism is even more difficult than, for instance, trying to comprehend a religion like 'Hinduism'.[13]

But this is a depressingly defeatist approach. If we are to understand the history, content and meaning of the belief systems commonly – and conveniently – labelled 'Gnosticism', then we must have a definition. So, for the purposes of this survey I propose to use a more recent description, given by Birger Pearson:

> In Gnosticism saving gnosis comes by revelation from a transcendent realm, mediated by a revealer who has come from that realm in order to awaken

---

[12] Michael Allen Williams, *Rethinking 'Gnosticism' An Argument for Dismantling a Dubious Category.* Princeton UP, 1996, p. 3.

[13] Karl W. Luckert, *Egyptian Light and Hebrew Fire.* Albany, 1991, p. 291.

Gnosticism and Gnosis: An Introduction

people to a knowledge of God and a knowledge of the true nature of the human self.... A characteristic feature of Gnosticism is a dualistic way of looking at God, humanity, and the world, involving a radical reinterpretation of earlier traditions. In terms of theology, the Gnostics split the transcendent God of the Bible into two: a super-transcendent supreme God who is utterly alien to the world, and a lower deity who is responsible for creating and governing the world in which we live.[14]

This is, I appreciate, unlikely to find favour with all, but let it suffice.

Having reached a definition, we must now consider the origins and nature of gnostic systems of belief. Where, when, how and why did those systems arise? How do the characteristic features of Gnosticism differ from those of the other faiths of its time and place? And what is the nature and content of the literary and other evidence that enables us to answer these questions?

---

14 Birger A. Pearson, *Ancient Gnosticism: Traditions and Literature*. Minneapolis, 2007, p. 12.

The Origins of Gnosticism and the Sources of Our Knowledge

Gnostic origins

For the Fathers of the early Church, the gnostics were heretics, infiltrating various false doctrines into the Church, and it was on this basis that they wrote their polemics against the many, disparate bodies of gnostics that they so busily catalogued and denigrated. Their view was largely accepted by church historians of the seventeenth to the nineteenth centuries, who drew all the varied 'gnostic' sects together under the single heading of Gnosticism. Such a simplistic view could not, however, stand up to the objective researches of the growing body of scholars, mostly in continental Europe, who, from the middle of the nineteenth century onwards, were applying detailed analysis and acute criticism to early Christian, Jewish and heterodox texts in their quest to understand the origins and earliest history of the Christian Church. As a consequence of their work we now have a much clearer view of gnostic origins, although it is still an incomplete picture and absolute certainty remains elusive – and probably unattainable.

Some early scholars (*e.g.* M. Friedländer) argued that Gnosticism grew up within heterodox Judaism in Ptolemaic Egypt. This approach was, however, overshadowed by the views

Gnosticism and Gnosis: An Introduction

of those who emphasised the significance of the dualist nature of Gnosticism and sought for its origins within overtly dualist religions. These scholars (*e.g.* W. Bousset and R. Reitzenstein) suggested Iranian dualism – Zoroastrianism and Mithraism – as the source of gnostic beliefs, but although there is, to a degree, a commonality of belief in opposing primal powers of light and darkness – of 'good' and 'evil' – present in both these religions and in most gnostic systems, explaining Gnosticism, as we understand it, in this way does not stand up to careful examination.

The most important point to consider is that the theology of neither Zoroastrianism nor Mithraism matches or parallels that of Gnosticism. It should also be borne in mind that one significant feature of Iranian religion is 'its insistence on the essential unity of body and soul ... as against the Indian and Gnostic view that soul and body are so radically different as to constitute two different worlds'.[1]

This belief in the unity of man is also characteristic of Judaism, and yet at the present time scholarly opinion about gnostic origins has returned to the view that 'gnostic' ideas were conceived and developed within heterodox Jewish communities in Egypt, and later in Palestine, during the last two centuries of the pre-Christian era. But while this is the prevailing view, not all contemporary scholars of Gnosticism subscribe to it. Some of them, but relatively few (e.g. E. Yamauchi and S. Pétrement) argue, in line with the Church Fathers, that gnostic schools of thought grew up within the early Christian Church and then

1 R.C. Zaehner, *The Dawn and Twilight of Zoroastrianism*. London, 1961 p. 274.

The Origins of Gnosticism

spread beyond it. Proponents of both of these approaches accept, as one would expect, that other influences, both Iranian and Neoplatonist, also played a role in the development of the various systematic forms of gnostic theology and cosmology.

Let us then consider the Jewish setting in which gnostic speculation and the different schools of gnostic thought that grew out of it, appear to have come into being. We must also take up the crucial questions of what are our sources of knowledge about the gnostics, how we should examine those sources (principally ancient texts, both of and about the gnostics), the form in which we have those source texts, and the circumstances under which they have been preserved and which have enabled us to have access to them.

The Jewish setting

After the time of the Babylonian exile, in the sixth century BC, many of the Jewish people did not return to Palestine but were 'scattered abroad' (the Diaspora) and established Jewish communities in North Africa, especially in Lower Egypt, and Asia Minor. Further migration took place during the fourth century, boosted by Jewish captives who were brought to Egypt after the Ptolemaic conquest of Palestine. Later generations of Jews also migrated to Egypt, to escape the wars and rebellions of the second century and even to provide troops for the Roman conquest of Egypt under Julius Caesar. But although the Jewish communities around Alexandria were well established and relatively prosperous, their aspiration to become integrated with the surrounding cultures could not be met without the loss, in no small measure, of their social and religious identity.

Gnosticism and Gnosis: An Introduction

For those Jews who sought to maintain their faith and to remain observant there was thus a considerable degree of cultural alienation and isolation from the surrounding Egyptian or Graeco-Roman society, although this was compensated for by continuing religious and cultural links with Palestine. Others, principally wealthy and literate Jews, began to develop new forms of understanding and interpreting the doctrines of Judaism – forms that had to take account of a perception that God, who had promised to deliver them from bondage, seemed to have deserted them. This led gradually to the rise of new forms of Jewish religious literature and also to the creation of a Greek translation of the Hebrew Torah: the Septuagint (so named for the supposed seventy translators).

Such religious and philosophical speculation resulted in a wealth of quasi-biblical texts that vary greatly in their quality and significance – and in the degree to which they depart from orthodoxy. Dependent on that degree, the surviving texts have been either appended to the Hebrew Bible or treated as something that, whatever their literary merit or historic interest, must be set aside from the canonical Scriptures. And as we examine their various forms and how they relate to gnostic texts, we must also make an excursus to consider the nature of the Canon of Scripture, of both the Old and the New Testaments.

The Canon: authoritative and unauthorised texts

The Canon of Scripture may be defined as the collection of writings that is accepted by believers of the Jewish and Christian faiths to be the divinely inspired, authoritative guide to doctrine

The Origins of Gnosticism

and rule of moral behaviour within their respective religious communities. However, not all of the texts now within the Canon have always been considered to have the same degree of inspiration.

The Hebrew Canon comprises the Torah (the Pentateuch: the first five books of the Bible), which constitutes the Jewish Law, and the prophetic, historical and poetical books. Apart from the Torah, which was accepted by all Jews, there were differences in the Hebrew and Greek texts of the other books – not all of which were accepted by such groups as the Sadducees or the Samaritans – and the final Canon was not determined until the end of the first century AD.

Establishing the Christian Canon was an even more contentious process. The early Church accepted most of the Hebrew Scriptures and gradually added distinctive Christian texts: the Synoptic Gospels, the Gospel of John, the Pauline Epistles and the Acts of the Apostles. But determining the Canon was a long process of careful sifting rather than an arbitrary act, and the initial collection of texts was not considered to be authoritative until the end of the second century. Even then it was neither definitive nor universally accepted: acceptance of the remaining books of the New Testament, as we know it today, took much longer and the familiar Canon was not agreed until late in the fourth century (and even later for the Revelation of St John). Nor was that the end of the matter, for universal agreement as to the inspiration and merit of every book of the Bible is still an unrealised goal, because some branches of the Church do not consider all of the Old Testament books to be inspired.

Gnosticism and Gnosis: An Introduction

Fig. 3　Hippolytus of Rome

The Origins of Gnosticism

These 'rejected' books are described variously as Apocrypha (from the Greek τα αποκρυφα, 'the hidden [things]') or Pseudepigrapha (Greek, 'writings with false superscription'; so called because they were ascribed to someone other than their real, and often unknown, author, in order to give them a greater authority). The fifteen Old Testament Apocrypha are treated as canonical by the Roman Catholic Church but are described as 'deuterocanonical' (*i.e.* accepted as canonical books at a later date than those in the Jewish Canon of Scripture), whereas the Anglican and Reformed Churches treat them as a non-essential supplement to the Old Testament.

The term 'Apocrypha' has also been applied to a variety of unorthodox early Christian texts that have traditionally found even less favour within the Church. There are some sixty of these texts that survive in substantial or complete form, plus many additional fragments, and which fall into the categories of Gospels, Acts, Epistles and Apocalypses. As with accepted New Testament texts they are attributed to one or more of the apostles, or to a prominent figure in the early Church, but even when these attributions are not clearly fictitious they are extremely improbable. Many of them also have an overt gnostic content, which accounts, in part, for their exclusion from the canonical New Testament.

Such texts might well merit the label of 'Pseudepigrapha', but the term is confined in practice to books that have been rigorously excluded from the Jewish Canon. The content of these books varies widely, but they can be categorised under five general headings: apocalyptic and related literature; testaments, mostly ascribed to the biblical patriarchs; expansions,

Gnosticism and Gnosis: An Introduction

sometimes legendary, of the Old Testament books; wisdom and philosophical literature; and prayers, psalms and odes, notably those ascribed to Solomon. Apocalypses – from the Greek word 'apocalypse' (ἀποκάλυψις), meaning a revelation, or unveiling – form the largest group and are concerned with revealing future events, specifically the last days of this world, when the righteous will be rewarded and the wicked punished. They also often include accounts of visionary journeys to and within supernatural worlds. To some extent visions of the future also occur in the various testaments, but these are more concerned with moral instruction for the present time.

Almost all of the Pseudepigrapha, in their original form, were the product of religious speculation within Jewish communities of the Diaspora from the third century BC to the second century AD and reflect the religious anxieties and confusion of those communities. But while they may depart from strict orthodoxy, their authors clearly remained within the broader bounds of Jewish faith and morals. Others did not, and in seeking for a spiritual explanation of their unhappy temporal state they either abandoned or drastically reinterpreted the dogmatic foundations – and sometimes the moral code – of their faith: perhaps the God of this world was not the true God.

The manner of this drift into dualism has been well expressed by the American scholar, Henry Green: 'For the disenfranchised Jewish intellectual the cosmic world alienated man from God and consequently God in turn became alien from the cosmic world.'[2] This is, of course, a modern interpretation of the textual evidence of Jewish speculative thought in the

2   Henry A. Green, *The Economic and Social Origins of Gnosticism*. Atlanta, GA, 1985, p. 203.

The Origins of Gnosticism

Graeco-Roman world, but there are other texts than Jewish Apocrypha and Pseudepigrapha that enable scholars to propose such interpretations and to speak with confidence about the nature and origins of Gnosticism. We also have texts that are our primary sources of knowledge and understanding of the gnostics; texts that contain both their words and those of their opponents. So let us consider the questions that arise: Who wrote these texts? When were they written? How trustworthy are they? And how have they been transmitted to us?

Knowledge of the gnosis

We gain our knowledge of the gnostics and their beliefs from two types of these ancient texts: those written about the gnostics by their contemporaries, and those written by, or ascribed to, the gnostics themselves. Of the first type the earliest known references to 'gnosis', either as desirable, illuminating knowledge or in a pejorative sense, and to individuals who would later be classified as gnostics, are found in the New Testament.

Thus 'the word of knowledge' [γνωσις] is presented by St Paul as one of the Gifts of the Spirit (1 Cor. 12:8) and as 'the treasures of wisdom and knowledge' [γνωσις] that are hidden in the mystery of Christ (Col. 2:3). Paul also warns Timothy against a different, false gnosis: 'Turn away from godless chatter and the opposing ideas of what is falsely called knowledge [γνωσις], which some have professed and in so doing have wandered from the faith' (1 Tim. 6:20). It is possible that when he issued this warning Paul had in mind the sorcerer Simon, whose story is told in the Acts of the Apostles (ch 8:9-24).

Gnosticism and Gnosis: An Introduction

This Simon had impressed the Samaritans as being 'the divine power known as the Great Power', but Philip's preaching mission had brought about his conversion to Christianity – which he clearly failed to understand. Later, when he sees Peter and John baptising in the Spirit, Simon offers them money to give him the same power 'so that everyone on whom I lay my hands may receive the Holy Spirit'. Peter roundly condemns him for his wickedness and folly, and Simon then seems to repent. But it is apparent from later and more detailed accounts of Simon, by the early Church Fathers, that he was perceived as a heretic and his apparent belief system can be construed as a form of proto-gnosticism. Nor was Simon alone in being seen as falling away from the faith – the Epistles of Paul and other apostles to the earliest Christian communities of the first century contain many strictures on those who were seen as deviating from the truth, in both doctrine and practice, although none of them can be certainly identified as being specifically gnostic.

But by the end of the first century, and throughout the second, the Fathers of the Church – the spiritual teachers who refined and systematised both Christian doctrine and church order – were cataloguing all the forms of false doctrine held by the various groups of heretics, *i.e.* those who had made the wrong choice about the Christian faith.[3] Whether or not we agree with the conclusions of the Fathers, and we must not forget that they were writing about people whom they saw as

---

3 The word 'heresy', from the Greek, αιρεσις (*haeresis*), means 'choice'; thus the heretic is one who has simply made a choice about his or her set of beliefs – religious, moral or political. In practice the word is applied to those who have chosen beliefs that run counter to the accepted creeds, the orthodoxy, of the currently dominant institutions.

The Origins of Gnosticism

their spiritual enemies, these early polemical texts formed the basis of our historical understanding of Gnosticism. A change of perspective did not become possible until the first discoveries of the second type of text in the late eighteenth century. Over the next 150 years further finds of papyri, mostly fragmentary, provided a meagre increase in the number of such texts and enabled a more informed view of the gnostics to develop, but it was not until 1945, and a final dramatic discovery, that our vision of Gnosticism and the gnosis would be completely changed.

The words of the Fathers

In the beginning there was no single Christian Church, only small communities of professing Christians. But as their numbers increased – and their small but distinct communities proliferated – so the need for both administrative structures and a generally agreed doctrinal position became more pressing. That this need was recognised before the end of the first century is clear from the content of the Pauline Epistles. However, broad agreement as to the true essence of Christian doctrine did not come about until three more centuries and a series of disputatious Ecclesiastical Councils – including the first two Oecumenical Councils that notionally represented the universal Church[4] – had passed and Christianity had become the official religion of the Roman Empire. Even then, significant differences remained, although the core of the Christian faith was not in dispute.

---

4   Seven Oecumenical Councils, the dogmatic pronouncements of which were, for the most part, accepted as binding by all branches of the Christian Church, were held before the breach between the Eastern and Western Churches in 1054. The first two such Councils were those of Nicaea (325 AD) and Constantinople (381 AD).

Gnosticism and Gnosis: An Introduction

Throughout this period, and beyond, Christian apologists and theologians – the Fathers of the Church – set out for the faithful what was to be believed and practised, and what was not. What they prescribed constituted orthodoxy and thus what dissented from that was heresy. Not all deviations from the faith were gnostic, but those that were considered to be so loom large in the polemical works of those Church Fathers who meticulously catalogued, analysed and fulminated against heresy in all its forms. We may not approve of their attitudes, but these accounts – making due allowance for demonising hyperbole – have proven to be accurate descriptions of the various gnostic schools of thought, and they are still an important source for our knowledge of the gnostics.

Eight of the Fathers, from Justin Martyr in the early second century to Augustine in the fourth, are particularly important in this respect and we shall make full use of their works in succeeding chapters. Here it is sufficient to note who they were, when they flourished and what they wrote. St. Justin Martyr (*c.*100–165 AD) was born at what is now Nablus in Samaria, and as a young man studied the major Greek philosophers. At the age of thirty he converted to Christianity and taught at Ephesus and then at Rome. He was an able apologist and wrote widely to refute pagan ideas and to establish a Christian philosophy. His principal surviving works promote Christian doctrines against the arguments of pagans and Jews, and in the *Dialogue with Trypho* (a Jewish apologist) he warns his readers against the doctrines of men 'who, in the name of Jesus, come and teach others atheistic and blasphemous doctrines and actions; we call them by the name of the originator of each false

The Origins of Gnosticism

doctrine'. He then names what he perceives to be the principal heretical schools – Marcionites, Valentinians, Basilidians and Saturnilians – most of which are now considered to be gnostic.

Justin did not, however, provide extensive accounts of these heresies. For that we must turn to the next generation, and to Irenaeus (c 130 – c 200 AD), who was not only a polemicist and theologian but also, for the last twenty years of his life, Bishop of Lyons. His principal work was *Adversus Haereses* (Against the Heretics), in which he gives detailed descriptions and full analyses of the doctrines of the gnostic sects, or movements, of the second century, together with a systematic refutation of these doctrines from a Christian perspective. It was then, and remained so until the nineteenth century, one of the most important sources of our knowledge of Gnosticism – informing scholarly opinion while simultaneously colouring it.

After Irenaeus came Clement of Alexandria, (*c.*150–*c.*215 AD), Tertullian, (*c.*160–*c.*225 AD) and Hippolytus, (*c.*170–*c.*236 AD), all of whom wrote extensively – but by no means exclusively – on gnostic and other heresies and philosophies. In his most significant work *Stromateis* (Miscellanies), Clement presents a Christian gnosis as being superior to that propounded in the various heretical sects. It is notable also that when Clement speaks of the major heretics (Valentinus, Marcion, Basilides, Cainites, Ophites etc.) he differs from the other Church Fathers in not referring to them as gnostics. But he is no less hostile to what he perceives as deviation from Christian truth.

Tertullian was a prolific author of theological works, most of which have survived. His writing is stylish and persuasive, and as a theologian he was much admired in the Church – if

Gnosticism and Gnosis: An Introduction

not among the gnostics, to whom he was implacably hostile. He wrote a general survey of gnostic ideas, 'Prescription against Heretics' (*De Praescriptione Haereticorum*), and a number of specific attacks upon major gnostic figures: notably Valentinus (*Adversus Valentinianos*) and Marcion, whom he refuted at very great length in his *Adversus Marcionem* – although while there is no question that Marcion was a heretic by orthodox standards he is not always classified as a gnostic.[5]

The controversial Alexandrian philosopher and theologian Origen (*c*.185–*c*.254 AD), considered Christians to be the true gnostics, but although he wrote a refutation of the anti-Christian work of the pagan philosopher Celsus, in which he also described and refuted various gnostic teachers, he did not produce systematic works against heresies in general. The important polemical text *Philosophumena* – now known as *The Refutation of all Heresies* – was formerly claimed as the work of Origen but is now definitively attributed to Hippolytus. As a source for the content of gnostic schools of thought it equals the work of Irenaeus in importance.

Two other later Church Fathers also provided significant studies of the gnostics and their successors. Epiphanius, (*c*.315 –403 AD), Bishop of Salamis, wrote the *Panarion* (Bread Basket) as a 'Refutation of all Heresies'. It is an uncritical and derivative attack upon every known heresy since the Church began, but it includes material that does not survive elsewhere about the gnostic and other heresies. More important by far are the works written against the Manichaeans by St Augustine

---

5 Here it should be noted that one text, 'Against all Heresies' (*Adversus Omnes Haereses*), that was formerly attributed to Tertullian is now considered to be almost certainly not his work.

The Origins of Gnosticism

(354 – 430 AD), the greatest of all of the patristic theologians. As a young man Augustine had been a follower of Mani, but after his conversion to Christianity he wrote against his former faith with the benefit of his first-hand experience.

To all these early, albeit hostile, sources for Gnosticism we should add one significant source from classical paganism: the opinions of the Neoplatonist philosopher, Plotinus ($c.$205–270 AD). That he did not think well of the gnostics is evident from the title of the ninth tractate of the second *Ennead*: 'Against the Gnostics; or Against Those that Affirm the Creator of the Cosmos and the Cosmos Itself to be Evil'. Plotinus approaches the gnostics as a philosopher. He sets out the essence of gnostic dualism, and then refutes it in depth from his Platonic viewpoint. His position is neatly summed up by A.D. Nock in these words: 'His argument, in brief, is that these Gnostics think very well of themselves and very ill of the universe.'[6] Thus far the opponents of Gnosticism. It would be 1,500 years later before the gnostics could again begin to speak for themselves.

Recovering the gnostic voice

Until late in the eighteenth century no manuscripts of gnostic texts were known to have survived the combination of destruction and neglect that followed the imposition of Christian orthodoxy upon the Roman world at the end of the fourth century. Then came two accidental finds. The first of these was made about 1750 when Dr. Anthony Askew (1722–74), a prominent classical scholar and collector of manuscripts, bought a Coptic manuscript, of unknown provenance, from a

---

6   A.D. Nock, *Essays on Religion and the Ancient World.* Oxford, 1972, p. 943.

Gnosticism and Gnosis: An Introduction

London bookseller. After his death it was acquired by the British Museum Library, but the two texts that the codex contains – *Pistis Sophia* and 'a part of the Books of the Saviour' – were not edited, published or translated (into Greek and Latin) until 1853, and no modern language translation appeared until the end of the century.

Equally slow was the publication of the second manuscript. This, also an ancient Coptic codex, was found in Upper Egypt at Medinet Habou, where it was purchased, in 1769, by the explorer James Bruce. At the sale of his manuscripts, in 1848, it was bought by the Bodleian Library, but nothing was published until 1892. This first publication, of the text and a German translation, was eventually followed, in 1933, by a complete facsimile text, comprising *The Books of Jeu* and 'The Untitled Text', with an English translation.

Further discoveries took place at the end of the 19th century. A third Coptic manuscript was discovered at Akhmim in Upper Egypt in 1896 and acquired for the Berlin Museum. It contains four gnostic texts, *The Gospel of Mary; Apocryphon of John; The Sophia of Jesus Christ*, and the *Acts of Peter*, which were published very gradually between 1903 and 1955. The first known gnostic material in Greek was discovered in 1896, again in Upper Egypt, among a large collection of papyri found at Oxyrhynchus. This consisted of fragments of *The Gospel of Thomas*, additional fragments of which were recovered later. All of these texts stimulated further study of the gnostics, but academic approaches to Gnosticism did not alter significantly until scholars began to appreciate the significance of another find, made in 1945.

The Origins of Gnosticism

In December of that year a large jar containing an unknown number of papyrus codices was unearthed by fellahin, digging for fertiliser near the town of Nag Hammadi in Upper Egypt. The codices were not at first recognised as having any value and some of them were burned. However, thirteen of them, containing a total of forty-nine gnostic texts – including many that were previously unknown – did survive and after years of alarms and diversions they are now in safe custody, twelve in the Coptic Museum at Cairo and one in the Jung Institute of Zurich. All of them have now been published as both texts and translations,[7] and other discoveries have followed, notably a copy of *The Gospel of Judas* that surfaced in 1983, with a very unclear provenance, and was finally published with much fanfare in 2006. The Nag Hammadi codices constitute a gnostic library and, precisely because they are gnostic and not the work of the opponents of Gnosticism, they are the single most important source for our understanding of Gnosticism. But have we succeeded in understanding it?

Translating knowledge into understanding

When the Egyptian fellahin discovered the jar containing the Nag Hammadi codices, they were wary about opening it as they feared that it might contain a *djinn* – an evil spirit – which 'could

---

7 All the known gnostic texts, those from Nag Hammadi and the few previously known codices, are now available in two publications from the publishers E.J. Brill of Leiden. There is a textual series, the Facsimile Edition of the Nag Hammadi Codices, and a long series of *Nag Hammadi Studies*, which includes both edited texts and translations, and critical studies of both these texts and the wider field of 'Gnostic Studies' in general. There is an admirable summary of the thirteen codices in Kurt Rudolph's book, *Gnosis* (1983). See pp. 44*ff*.

Gnosticism and Gnosis: An Introduction

cause trouble if released from the jar'.[8] But open it they did and trouble surely followed, not from supernatural beings but from decades of continuing squabbles among scholars in the field of gnostic studies. These have arisen not so much because of disputes over establishing definitive texts and translations of the codices – over which there is substantial agreement – but rather over questions of interpretation of the texts and determining what light they throw on the concept of 'Gnosticism', and on the nature and development of early Christianity: its foundation texts, the establishment of the Canon of Scripture, and its relationships with the other religions amongst which it, and the various gnostic sects, were born and came to maturity.

Nor are these disputes insignificant. Some of the more vocal scholars working with the gnostic scriptures have been led to question our very definition of Christianity, or Christianities as they would prefer to say, and have suggested that these texts require us radically to redefine just what Christianity is. However, it is important to bear in mind that these are matters of scholarly opinion and debate, not of indisputable fact. The discovery of the Nag Hammadi codices has unquestionably led to a revolution in our knowledge and understanding of Gnosticism, and it has led some biblical scholars to view the gnostics in a more favourable light as they have gained increasing access to gnostic writings. But we would do well to be impartial as we improve our understanding of the gnostics. Christian scholars should not be combative, for these new texts have not, in any sense, undermined the Christian faith, and those tempted

---

8 M. Meyer (Ed.), *The Nag Hammadi Scriptures*. New York, 2007, p. 3. Quoting James M. Robinson.

The Origins of Gnosticism

to do so should not perceive the gnostics as unalloyed paragons of virtue, nor look upon the Church Fathers who opposed them as double-dyed villains. Truth, whatever it may be perceived to be, is never that simple.

We are now equipped with adequate means to work towards establishing an objective and true understanding of the phenomenon of Gnosticism that could, but probably will not, be acceptable to a broad consensus of scholars. Such a goal was not possible in previous centuries and it was, in any event, as unsought as it was unlikely.

Because of the absence of their original texts, and a perception of them as being of little significance, there was little scholarly interest in the gnostics before the nineteenth century, and even then there was no determined attempt to understand them. Attempts at systematic, critical analysis of Gnosticism was reserved to such controversial theologians as F.C. Baur and August Neander, whose concern was with its role in shaping the early Church. The first new approach to Gnosticism was proposed by Jacques Matter, a French Protestant scholar with a deep and sympathetic interest in esoteric speculation. In his book *Histoire critique du Gnosticisme* (1828), Matter suggested that Gnosticism developed from Jewish kabbalism and Iranian dualism, and he argued that gnostic systems should be classified not on the basis of types of philosophical speculation, but on the regions – Syria, Egypt and Asia Minor – in which the various gnostic schools had been established.

Matter's approach had no influence in academic circles, but his enthusiasm for the pictorial imagery of Gnosticism – the ancient engraved gems that were then believed to be of gnostic

Gnosticism and Gnosis: An Introduction

origin – was reflected in the first popular work on the gnostics in English, C.W. King's *The Gnostics and Their Remains* (1864). Although King was an authority on ancient gems, his knowledge of the gnostics and their milieu was limited to patristic sources and to the speculations on Classical Paganism of the Romantic Era. His book was thus of little critical value and did little to advance our understanding of Gnosticism.

The first significant effort to gain a true perception came at the end of the nineteenth century, when the publication of original gnostic texts, few though they were, made it possible for scholars to reconsider their interpretation of Gnosticism and to evaluate objectively its possible role in the early development of Christianity. Independent scholars with a penchant for esotericism, such as G.R.S. Mead, began also to present Gnosticism as a philosophy and faith superior to orthodox Christianity. This, however, required them to make hostile value judgements on the reliability of patristic sources and, although the wider setting of the early Church was beginning to be studied in depth, gnostic ideas and presumed practices were perceived in the academic world rather as degenerate than noble.

At the same time growing scholarly enthusiasm for comparative religion did bring greater attention to Gnosticism as a religious phenomenon, and some theologians – notably Walter Baur[9] – argued that making a clear-cut distinction between orthodoxy and heresy in the early Church, in which orthodoxy was ill-defined, is impossible. But the scarcity of gnostic writings made any thorough reappraisal of Gnosticism

---

9   Baur's seminal work, *Orthodoxy and Heresy in Earliest Christianity*, was published in 1934, although the English translation did not appear until 1971.

The Origins of Gnosticism

itself equally difficult. Only after the contents of the Nag Hammadi library became gradually available to scholars in its entirety could Gnosticism begin to be properly studied, and the availability of the texts certainly stimulated scholarly enthusiasm. They also stimulated debate, and sometimes rancorous debate, as is the way with all contentious material. But we are at last en route to what we might justly describe as the solution of the gnostic problem.

How long it will take to arrive at that destination cannot be assessed with any accuracy – the more so given the apparent propensity for scholars to engage in unseemly disputes, and occasionally in outright deception[10] – but we can at last anticipate such an achievement.

And while we wait it is only proper that the intelligent non-specialist reader should be enabled to draw his or her own conclusions about the gnostics and their beliefs. So let us enter the world of the gnostics, setting down the beliefs and practices of gnostic systems and schools of thought, illustrating specific ideas from the words of both the gnostics themselves and their opponents, and considering the principal varieties of Gnosticism.

---

10   The classic example of scholarly fraud in this field is the so-called 'Secret Gospel of Mark'. This supposed gospel text consisted of an extract contained in what was alleged to be a late copy of a previously unknown letter of St Clement of Alexandria. This forgery, which it has been shown conclusively to be, was perpetrated, for reasons connected with his private life, by a respected biblical scholar, Morton Smith. See below, p. 121.

Gnostics and Their Teachers: Systems of Gnostic Belief

When speaking of gnostic beliefs it must always be borne in mind that Gnosticism is a modern term, that there was never a discrete, identifiable 'gnostic religion' as such – still less any over-arching 'Gnostic Church' – and that the term 'gnostic' is a convenient adjective to apply to a group of religious movements, with certain defining characteristics in common, that arose and developed within the approximate boundaries of the Roman Empire.

The earliest forms of these gnostic religious beliefs are generally accepted as having originated within dissident communities of the Jewish Diaspora, especially in Egypt and Palestine, but clearly identifiable gnostic systems did not appear until the rise of Jewish Christian communities in these and other regions of the empire, notably Syria, Asia Minor and Rome itself, during the second half of the first century of the Christian era.

Gnostic systems expanded in number, complexity and sophistication during the second century, and by c.200 AD the most significant forms of gnostic faith – if such a term may justly be used – were well established. But the great majority of the founders and teachers of gnostic religious systems, and their followers, did not identify themselves as adherents of a 'gnostic

Gnostics and Their Teachers

religion'. In their own eyes they were Christian, although this is not at all how the orthodox Church perceived them.

But what is orthodoxy? The earliest Christian communities varied greatly from one another in their doctrinal positions on such issues as the person of Christ, the meaning of salvation, the nature and attainment of the Kingdom of God, and what constituted Scripture. There was not, and still is not, complete agreement on every doctrinal issue across the entire spectrum of the Christian faith, but agreement in principle on the major points of doctrine was achieved at the Council of Nicaea in 325 AD. At this council a profession of faith, in a form of words that was effectively universally acceptable, was formulated for the first time. This was the Nicene Creed, which, in the longer and more detailed version agreed at the later Council of Constantinople, in 381 AD, has remained in use throughout the Christian world, substantially in these words:

> I believe in one God, the Father Almighty, Maker of heaven and earth, and of all things visible and invisible. And in one Lord Jesus Christ, the only-begotten Son of God, begotten of the Father before all worlds; God of God, Light of Light, very God of very God; begotten, not made, being of one substance with the Father, by whom all things were made. Who, for us men for our salvation, came down from heaven, and was incarnate by the Holy Spirit of the virgin Mary, and was made man; and was crucified also for us under Pontius Pilate; He suffered and was buried; and the third day He rose again, according to the Scriptures; and ascended into heaven, and sits on the right hand of the Father; and He shall come again, with glory, to

Gnosticism and Gnosis: An Introduction

judge the quick and the dead; whose kingdom shall have no end. And I believe in the Holy Ghost, the Lord and Giver of Life; who proceeds from the Father [and the Son]; who with the Father and the Son together is worshipped and glorified; who spoke by the prophets. And I believe in one holy catholic and apostolic Church. I acknowledge one baptism for the remission of sins; and I look for the resurrection of the dead, and the life of the world to come. Amen.

Thus was the Christian Church finally provided with an authorised statement of the essential features of its faith to the satisfaction of all of its branches.[1] But not to that of the gnostics.

Not that all gnostics considered themselves to be Christian. We know from studies of the Nag Hammadi codices that some gnostic texts have no Christian content at all, and were presumably created and used by members of non-Christian religious communities. To such gnostics the Nicene Creed, and the associated anathemas of the Church, would have been irrelevant, but the philosophical concepts, the mythology and the cosmology that underpinned almost all of the various forms of gnostic expression were common to Christian and non-Christian gnostic alike. So, what were these defining features of Gnosticism, the world-view that determined what gnostics believed and how they lived? And first, what exactly did 'gnosis' mean to them?

---

1 The divisive *filioque* (and the Son) clause, in relation to the procession of the Holy Spirit, does not appear in the Nicene Creeds of 325 or 381 AD. It was an interpolation of the late sixth century that came into general use in the West about 800 AD, but it was never accepted by the Eastern Churches

Gnostics and Their Teachers

Gnostics were what their name implies: 'knowers', but theirs was not intellectual knowledge. It was a religious understanding, a revealed awareness of spiritual reality that contained within it the means of the gnostics' salvation from the limitation and misery of the material world. Kurt Rudolph, one of the most perceptive expositors of Gnosticism, noted that,

> It is a knowledge given by revelation, which has been made available only to the elect who are capable of receiving it, and therefore has an esoteric character. This knowledge freely bestowed can extend from the basic insight into the divine nature of man, his origin and his destiny, up to a complete system.[2]

Before we come to the nature of man, however, we must first consider the most significant element in the gnostic world-view: the nature of God. For the orthodox Christian there is only one God, only one Creator, whose creation is good. Against this the gnostic set a dualist conception of God. In this religious dualism the transcendent God – the One, remote and unknowable – exists in the Pleroma (fullness), a state of being that is 'the totality of unmanifest qualities of the Godhead'.[3] From this supreme God all else emanates. In the words of Irenaeus, as he sets out the system of the gnostic teacher Valentinus,

> he exists in the invisible and ineffable heights a pre-existent, perfect aeon, whom [the Valentinians] also

---

[2] Kurt Rudolph, *Gnosis, the Nature and History of an Ancient Religion.* Edinburgh, 1983, p. 55.

[3] Violet Macdermot, 'The Concept of Pleroma in Gnosticism', in M. Krause (Ed.), *Gnosis and Gnosticism. Papers read at the Eighth International Conference on Patristic Studies, Oxford ... 1979.* Leiden, 1981, p. 76.

Gnosticism and Gnosis: An Introduction

call Pre-beginning, Forefather, and Primal Cause (Bythos), that he is inconceivable and invisible, eternal and uncreated and that he existed in great peace and stillness in unending aeons.[4]

Gnostic dualism is, however, unusual in that it views the non-material, spiritual world as good but treats the visible, material world of matter as irredeemably evil. This separates it completely from Iranian dualism, in which there are equal and opposite gods of good and evil, and Platonic dualism, which sets the eternal world of the One over the finite world; neither of these forms rejects matter as being essentially evil. Indeed, it is this aspect of gnostic thought that Plotinus attacks when he writes,

> Nor would it be sound to condemn the Cosmos as less than beautiful, as less than the noblest possible in the corporeal; and neither can any charge be laid against its source. The world, we must reflect, is a product of Necessity, not of deliberate purpose: it is due to a higher Kind engendering in its own likeness by a natural process.[5]

And this Neoplatonic view was, in its turn, anathema to the gnostics. The gnostic view was that within the Pleroma the transcendent God undergoes a process of self-realisation, which results in a complex series of pairs of qualities and attributes: heavenly beings – the aeons – that emanate or unfold from him. The first of these emanations is female, Ennoia (Thought), or

4 Irenaeus, *Adversus Haereses*, I:1. Translation adapted from Rudolph, *op. cit.*, p. 62. The term 'aeon' is used in the sense of both a supernatural being and an age.

5 Plotinus, *The Enneads*. (III.2, 3.) Translated by Stephen McKenna. London, 3rd ed, 1962, pp. 162-163.

Gnostics and Their Teachers

Barbelo; with her the transcendent God generates Light, or Autogenes. Then follow further successive pairs that variously unite and separate in descending levels until a final aeon, Sophia (wisdom), is produced.

Sophia desires to create a being herself, apart from the divine Pleroma and without divine authority, and so gives birth to the evil Demiurge (Greek δημιουργός, craftsman or artisan), who, ignorant of his divine origin and in unknowing imitation of the divine realm, fashions the worlds of matter – the Earth and the material heavens above it – and populates them with archons (rulers), angels, humans and all lesser forms of life.

Inevitably, this very brief summary cannot do justice to the gnostic vision of the descent of creation from the sublime realm of the One to the evil-infected world of matter. Much fuller expositions are given by heresiologists, such as Irenaeus and Hippolytus, and in original gnostic texts. Both types of account are valuable and informative sources for our understanding of gnostic doctrines, but they differ in their flavour. The Church Fathers were writing polemics but, although we must take account of their disapproving tone, there is no reason to doubt their factual accuracy. On the other hand gnostic authors were presenting their texts to believers, and while they are difficult, there is a poetic feel to them. They vary greatly in detail, as do the descriptions of the Fathers, but an example of each type will be adequate to illustrate gnostic cosmogony in the language of its time.

One of the most complex accounts of the descent of Sophia is given in *The Apocryphon of John*, from which these extracts are taken:

Gnosticism and Gnosis: An Introduction

And [the transcendent God's] thinking produced something ... the perfect forethought of the entirety ... the image of the perfect invisible virgin spirit. This is the power, the glory of the Barbelo, the most perfect glory among the aeons ... It is the first thinking of the spirit's image.

It [the Barbelo] became a womb for the entirety, for it was prior to all others, being the mother-father, the first human being, the holy spirit, the thrice-male, the three powers; the thrice-androgynous name; and was the most eternal aeon among the invisible.

[The Barbelo, forethought, then requests and obtains, successively, prognosis, incorruptibility, eternal life and truth.] This is the androgynous quintet of aeons, that is, the group of ten aeons, which constitutes the parent.

And it gazed at the Barbelo ... and the Barbelo conceived by it, and it begot a luminous spark consisting of light that was blessed, though not equal to its parent's magnitude. This was the only-begotten offspring of the mother-father which appeared, and the mother-father's only begetting; it was the only-begotten of the parent, the uncontaminated light.

[This spark is then anointed by the invisible spirit and from it come four luminaries and twelve eternal realms, the last of which is Sophia (wisdom), who then produces an image within herself – without the spirit's will.]

Gnostics and Their Teachers

And out of her was shown forth an imperfect product, that was different from her manner of appearance, for she had made it without her consort. And compared to the image of its mother it was misshapen, having a different form.

Now, when she saw that her desired artefact was stamped differently – serpentine, with a lion's face, and with its eyes gleaming like flashes of lightning – she cast it outside of her ... so that none of the immortals might see it ... And she surrounded it with a luminous cloud. And she put a throne in the midst of the cloud, so that no being might see it except for the holy spirit called "mother of the living". And she called its name Ialtabaoth.

[This 'first ruler', the demiurge, unaware of its true nature, then engenders a series of rulers, and finally creates the material universe.]

And seeing the creation surrounding it and the multitude of angels around it that has come to exist out of it, it said to them, "For my part, I am a jealous god. And there is no other god apart from me." In uttering this it signified to the angels staying with it that another god did exist. For if no other one existed, of whom would it be jealous ?[6]

Irenaeus, in his *Adversus Haereses*, gives an even longer, more detailed and somewhat different account of gnostic cosmogony from the school of Valentinus. It is more prosaic than the

---

6 Bentley Layton, *The Gnostic Scriptures: A New Translation with Annotations and Introductions*. London, 1987. See pp. 30-38.

Gnosticism and Gnosis: An Introduction

gnostic texts and two extracts, concerning the first and last stages as given above, are enough to indicate its style and tone:

> Once upon a time Bythos [the Primal Cause] determined to produce from himself the beginning of all things and, like a seed, he deposited this production which he had resolved to bring forth, as in a womb, in that Sige who was with him. She then, on receiving his seed, became pregnant and gave birth to Nous, who was both like and equal to him who produced him, and who alone comprehended the greatness of his father. [I.1, 1]
>
> They say that the Demiurge believed that he had created all this of himself, but in fact he had made them because Achamoth [Sophia] prompted him. He made the heaven without knowing the heaven; he formed man without knowing him; he brought the earth to light without knowing it. And, in every case, they say, he was ignorant of the ideas of the things he made, and even of his own mother, and imagined that he alone was all things.[7] [I.5, 3]

Such was the gnostics' conception of the creation of the spiritual worlds and of the descent into matter, but where, in all this, is humanity? What exactly is man, and how does this grand cosmogonic scheme relate to the fate of the individual gnostic ? According to the classic gnostic myth, man was created by the Demiurge, but trapped within him – but not within every human being – there is a spiritual seed, a fragment of the divine spark, that is waiting to be rescued by the divine Saviour. One

---

7 Irenaeus, *Adversus Haereses*. In Werner Foerster, *Gnosis, a Selection of Gnostic Texts. I. Patristic Evidence.* Oxford, 1972, pp. 127 & 136.

succinct description of how this came about is given by Clement of Alexandria, quoting the Valentinian gnostic, Theodotus:

> The Valentinians say that when the psychic body had been formed a male seed was implanted by the Logos in the elect soul while it slept, which is the effluence deriving from the angels, in order that there may be no deficiency.
>
> And this operated like leaven, in that it unified what appeared to be separated, namely, the soul and the flesh, which had in fact been brought forth separately by Sophia. Sleep was for Adam the oblivion of the soul, which the spiritual seed, implanted by the Saviour in the soul, held together in order that it should not be dissolved.[8]

There are, however, three types of man, described thus in the gnostic text *On the Origin of the World*:

> Now the first Adam, (Adam) of Light, is spirit-endowed (*pneumatikos*), and appeared on the first day. The second Adam is soul-endowed (*psykhikos*), and appeared on the sixth day, which is called Aphrodite. The third Adam is a creature of the earth (*khoikos*), that is, the man of the law, and he appeared on the eighth day ... the tranquillity (*anapausis*) of poverty, which is called Sunday (*hēmera Hēliou*).
>
> And the progeny of the earthly Adam became numerous and was completed, and produced within

---

8 Clement of Alexandria, *Excerpta ex Theodoto*, I, 2, 1-2. In Foerster, *op. cit.* I, pp. 222-223.

itself every kind of scientific information of the soul-endowed Adam. But all were in ignorance.[9]

The distinction between these three types is that the spiritual man (*pneumatikos*) is pre-destined to salvation; the soul man (*psykhikos*) can be saved, if he acts according to the will of the transcendent God; but the purely material man (*khoikos* or *hylikos*) cannot be saved and must die. In most gnostic systems salvation for the spiritual man and the soul man is mediated by Jesus Christ by way of the power vested in him: 'So when the Saviour came, he awakened the soul, but kindled the spark. For the words of the Lord are power' (*Excerpta ex Theodoto*, 3, 1). And the risen Christ alone can restore the sparks of light to the Pleroma:

> The Cross is a symbol of Limit in the Pleroma, for it divides the unfaithful from the faithful, just as the latter separates the world from the Pleroma. Therefore Jesus, by the sign of the Cross, also carries the seeds on his shoulders, and leads them into the Pleroma. For Jesus is called 'the shoulders of the seed', but the head is called Christ.[10]

The essence of the return to the Pleroma is given in *The Gospel of Philip*:

> It is from water and fire that the soul and the spirit came into being. It is from water and fire and light that the son of the bridal chamber [came into being]. The fire is the chrism, the light is the fire.

---

9   From *On the Origin of the World*, translated by Hans-Gebhard Bethge and Bentley Layton, in Bentley Layton (Ed.), *Nag Hammadi Codex II, 2-7*. Volume Two, Leiden, 1989, p.71.

10 Clement of Alexandria, *op. cit.*, 42, 1, p. 229.

Gnostics and Their Teachers

> I am not referring to that fire which has no form, but to the other fire whose form is white, which is bright and beautiful, and which gives beauty.
>
> Truth did not come into the world naked, but it came in types and images. The world will not receive truth in any other way. There is a rebirth and an image of rebirth. It is certainly necessary to be born again through the image. Which one? Resurrection. The image must rise again through the image. The bridal chamber and the image must enter through the image into the truth: this is the restoration. Not only must those who produce the name of the father and the son and the holy spirit do so, but also those who have produced them for you. If one does not acquire them the name ('Christian') will also be taken from him. But one receives them in the unction of … the power of the cross. This power the apostles called 'the right and the left' – For this person is no longer a Christian but a Christ. The lord did everything in a mystery, a baptism and a chrism and a eucharist and a redemption and a bridal chamber.[11]

Baptism alone, however, is not enough; there is still the overriding need for knowledge, as emphasised by Theodotus:

> It is not the bath [baptism] alone that makes us free, but also the knowledge: who were we? what have we become? where were we? into what place have we been cast? whither are we hastening?

---

11   From *The Gospel According to Philip*, 67. Translated by Wesley W. Isenberg, in Bentley Layton (Ed.), *Nag Hammadi Codex II, 2-7*. Volume One, Leiden, 1989, pp. 175 & 177.

Gnosticism and Gnosis: An Introduction

from what are we delivered? what is birth? what is rebirth?[12]

Armed with this knowledge the gnostic can then engage with the necessary ritual procedures – prayers and invocations, as given by Jesus to his disciples. One impressive example of such a proceeding is given in the late gnostic text, *Pistis Sophia*:

> And while Jesus said this, Thomas, Andrew, James and Simon the Canaanite were in the west with their faces turned to the east, and Philip and Bartholomew were in the south turned towards the north, and the rest of the disciples and the women-disciples stood behind Jesus. But Jesus stood at the altar.
>
> And Jesus made invocation, turning himself towards the four corners of the world with his disciples, who were all clad in linen garments, and saying: '*iaō iaō iaō*.' This is its interpretation: *iōta*, because the universe hath gone forth; *alpha*, because it will turn itself back again; *ōmega*, because the completion of all the completeness will take place.
>
> And when Jesus had said this, he said: '*iaphtha iaphtha mounaēr mounaēr ermanouēr ermanouēr ermanouēr.*' That is: 'O Father of all fatherhoods of the boundless spaces, hear me for the sake of my disciples whom I have led before thee, that they may have faith in all the words of thy truth, and grant all for which I shall invoke thee; for I

---

12 Clement of Alexandria, *op. cit.*, 78, 2, p. 230.

Gnostics and Their Teachers

know the name of the Father of the Treasury of the Light.[13]

In the *Gospel of Thomas*, Jesus identified himself as the light and tells his disciples how they are to identify themselves to the world:

> Jesus said, "It is I who am the light which is above them all. It is I who am the all. From me did the all come forth, and unto me did the all extend. Split a piece of wood, and I am there. Lift up the stone and you will find me there." [Saying 77]

> Jesus said, "If they say to you, 'Where did you come from ?', say to them, 'We came from the light, the place where the light came into being on its own accord and established itself and became manifest through their image.' If they say to you, 'Is it you ?', say, 'We are its children, and we are the elect of the living father.' If they ask you, 'What is the sign of your father in you ?', say to them, 'It is movement and repose.' " [Saying 50][14]

Gnostics, however, still lived among the inhabitants of the material world, from which there was no immediate escape. How they lived while the divine spark within them was encased with matter depended on the moral code they accepted. For most 'Christian' gnostics this was the morality laid down by Jesus

---

13   G.R.S. Mead, (Trans.) *Pistis Sophia, a Gnostic Miscellany: Being for the Most Part Extracts from the Books of the Saviour.* Rev. ed. 1921, pp. 295-296 (Book Five).

14   From *The Gospel of Thomas*, translated by Thomas O. Lambdin, in James M. Robinson, *The Nag Hammadi Library in English*. Third, completely revised edition. San Francisco, 1988, pp. 135 & 132.

Gnosticism and Gnosis: An Introduction

Christ, but the belief that matter is evil and that the creator of the material world – the Demiurge, whom they identified with the God of the Law – is also evil, suggested to some of those who believed themselves to be 'spiritual seeds' (*pneumatikoi*) that they were freed from all constraints of the moral law. Whether many gnostics took up this amoral interpretation of the Christian concept of the 'Freedom of the Gospel' and led actively libertine lives is unclear. There are no known gnostic libertine texts, and the accusations of libertinism are found only in the works of the Church Fathers – and in few enough of those.

Irenaeus refers to some Valentinians preparing a 'bridal chamber' for a ceremonial, spiritual marriage (which is also referred to in the *Gospel of Philip*), but there is no suggestion that this was a sexual act. Only Epiphanius makes claims to extensive libertine behaviour among groups of gnostics, accusing some of them not only of holding orgies but also of cannibalism (*Panarion* XXVI). But his reports are from the late fourth century and it may be noted that one major gnostic text, *Pistis Sophia*, of which the surviving copies are from the fifth century – and were thus circulating among the later gnostics – expressly condemns orgiastic behaviour (*Pistis Sophia*, 147: Those who commit the worst forms of sexual perversion 'will be consumed and perish in the outer darkness', to be 'destroyed and dissolved'). We may reasonably conclude that gnostics, as individuals, accepted conventional mores and were neither more nor less morally upright than their orthodox Christian contemporaries.

Gnostics and Their Teachers

Given their concern with ensuring that they did have true gnosis – the saving knowledge that would awaken the spark within them and enable them to negotiate safely the difficult way of return to the Pleroma – gnostics were most likely to have spent the time dedicated to their faith in learning from their teachers the precise details of the process of ascent through the heavens. In some gnostic schools they were aided in this by diagrams and symbolic designs that both mapped the heavens and provided them with the secret seals that they would need to overcome hostile supernatural beings.

There is a very long series of such diagrams in *The Books of Jeu*, a gnostic text of the third century that is a part of the Bruce Codex. These form a part of the detailed and complex instructions delivered by Jesus to his disciples so that they are aware of the many regions, or 'treasuries', of the Pleroma and the manner in which they will be able to rise through the aeons, overcome the archons (rulers) of the aeons and thus pass into and through the series of treasuries.

The schematic diagrams represent the various treasuries and reveal the specific form of the name of Jeu (the supreme God) within each treasury, together with the character – a symbolic seal that represents him – and the names of the three 'watchers' and twelve 'emanations' of that treasury. In addition to this, Jesus also teaches his disciples the correct procedure for progressing through the successive aeons, giving them the name (to be spoken), the pictorial symbol (with which to seal oneself), the number (to be shown) and the appropriate secret names, or words of power, for each. The archons will then draw back and the disciple may continue his journey.

Gnosticism and Gnosis: An Introduction

A different, and more complex cosmological diagram, apparently used by the gnostic Ophites, is described in detail by Origen, in his book, *Contra Celsum*.[15] He was not impressed by the diagram, which he found to be 'completely unconvincing', and argued that neither the Ophites – 'a most undistinguished sect' in his opinion – nor Celsus[16] himself, who used the diagram in his argument as to the folly of Christianity, truly understood the scripturally based doctrines of the Christian faith. But the gnostics thought otherwise, and the various processes by which they sought to return to the Pleroma remained of crucial importance to them – to such an extent that some of them developed a form of baptism to be used at the point of death, to ensure the ascent of the departing soul.

Irenaeus describes such a process, although he does not specify the specific gnostic school concerned, in which they 'continue to redeem persons even up to the moment of death, by placing on their heads oil and water'[17] while using various invocations that will give them power over the inhabitants of the aeons. He does not specify the form of baptism, but it was presumably similar to that given in the preceding section:

> Into the name of the unknown Father of the universe – into truth, the mother of all things – into Him who descended on Jesus – into union, and redemption, and communion with the powers.[18]

15 Origen, *Contra Celsum*. Translated with an Introduction & Notes by Henry Chadwick. Cambridge, 1953, VI, 24-31. See pp. 337-348.

16 Celsus was an Epicurean philosopher of the late second century AD. Origen's work was designed to refute the arguments in Celsus's book *The True Word* (Λόγος Αληθης), which was an attack on Christianity.

17 Irenaeus, *Adversus Haereses*. I. 21, 5. Translated by Alexander Roberts and W.H. Rambaut. Edinburgh, 1868, p. 83.

18 *ibid. I.* 21, 3. p. 82.

Gnostics and Their Teachers

The departing soul is given the appropriate words by which he will overcome the archons. He will assert his own superiority over them, but first he tells them who he is and whence he comes:

> I am a son from the Father – the Father who had a pre-existence, and a son in Him who is pre-existent. I have come to behold all things, both those which belong to myself and others, although, strictly speaking, they do not belong to others, but to Achamoth, who is female in nature, and made these things for herself. For I derive from Him who is pre-existent, and I come again to my own place whence I went forth.[19]

Prayers, invocations and ceremonial forms such as these are found in both gnostic texts and in the polemical works of the Church Fathers, but the specific content varies from school to school. And there were many gnostic schools of thought, varying in specific doctrines while sharing an underlying dualism and building upon a broadly similar creation and salvation myth. Many of the gnostic belief systems perceived themselves as being Christian but, unlike the orthodox forms of Christianity, no one gnostic school came to hold a dominant position over the others. Nor did any of them triumph over orthodoxy.

One reason for this was their elitist nature, which did not favour evangelism, but another was their perceived – and often real – origin in the teaching of charismatic individuals, whose names came to be identified with specific gnostic schools. We know them from the catalogues produced by the major heresiologists, but it is important to recognise that not all

19   *ibid. I.* 21, 5. pp. 83-84.

Gnosticism and Gnosis: An Introduction

heresies were then, or would be now, considered to be 'gnostic' in their nature. The number varies from twelve of those listed by Irenaeus to twenty-six of the eighty heresies in Epiphanius's *Panarion*. Of these the earliest are placed in sub-apostolic times but the majority appear in the second century.

In a limited space it is impossible to survey all of them,[20] but we may consider briefly the defining characteristics of the most significant schools, as seen by themselves and by their opponents.

Gnostic teachers and what they taught

Simon Magus and his followers

The early Church Fathers looked upon Simon Magus as the first, and possibly the worst, gnostic teacher among many, but from what is known of his life and doctrines – mostly from Justin Martyr and Irenaeus – he seems to have been more of a charismatic wonder-worker than a teacher of gnosis, and more spiritual opportunist than magician. Nonetheless, he scandalised the early Christian communities both by his antinomian hostility to the Mosaic Law and by his presumption of spiritual power. He set out a more or less standard form of the gnostic cosmogony, and added the novel features of presenting himself as divine and claiming that his partner, Helena, was 'the first conception of his mind, the mother of all, by whom, in the beginning, he conceived in his mind the thought of forming angels and archangels.'[21]

---

20 The full lists of the heresiologists are given in Williams, *op. cit.*, pp. 34-35. For an excellent brief survey of the different named gnostic systems, see Kurt Rudolph, *op. cit.*, pp. 294-325.

21 Irenaeus, *op. cit.*, I. 23, 2. p. 87.

Gnostics and Their Teachers

Simon probably died about 70 AD but accounts of his life are almost entirely legendary. He does seem to have travelled to Rome and he did gain numerous followers, which explains the rancour of the Fathers when writing about him. The Simonian School, if such it may be called, persisted through the second century and it was probably these later followers who compiled the material in *The Great Exposition* (Αποφασις Μεγαλη), a work ascribed to Simon by Hippolytus, who used it to describe his cosmogony and doctrine of salvation – including Simon's rejection of the Law. This, says Hippolytus, has led his followers to 'do what they will as being free'.

> For they claim they have been saved by his [*i.e.* Simon's] grace. For no one is liable to judgment if he does anything evil; for evil exists not by nature but by law. For he says it is the angels who made the world who made the Law whatever they wished, thinking to enslave those who hearkened to them. And again they say that (there will be) a dissolution of the world for the redemption of their own men.

> Therefore the disciples of this (man) practise magic arts and incantations, and send out love-philtres and charms and the demons called dream-bringers for the troubling of whom they will.[22]

To what extent Simonians really *were* libertines and magicians we do not know, but he did establish a school that was perceived as a threat to some Christian communities and thus called for a degree of demonisation. But his succession – Menander,

---

22 Hippolytus, *Philosophumena or the Refutation of all Heresies* ... Translated by F. Legge. London, 1921, Bk. 6, 19-20. (Vol. 2, p. 16)

Gnosticism and Gnosis: An Introduction

Saturnilus and Basilides – could not be branded as antinomian, although they propounded more obviously gnostic systems.

Menander, who flourished in the late first century, was Simon's immediate successor. He claimed to be the divine saviour sent forth by the 'primary Power', and brought salvation by baptism: 'for his disciples obtain the resurrection by being baptised into him, and can die no more, but remain in the possession of immortal youth.' [23] Like Simon, Menander was a Samaritan, but he taught in Antioch where Saturninus (or Satornilos) became his pupil. He, in turn, developed another expression of the gnostic myth, in which the Jewish God is one of seven angels, subordinate creators of the material world but hostile to the supreme God.

The Saviour, Christ, was not born as man but was 'without birth, without body, and without figure, but was, by supposition, a visible man'. Further,

> because all the powers wished to annihilate his father, Christ came to destroy the God of the Jews, but to save such as believe in him; that is, those who possess the spark of his life. This heretic was the first to affirm that two kinds of men were formed by the angels – the one wicked, and the other good.[24]

Thus, as the second century unfolded, what would become essential gnostic doctrines were being developed.

---

23 Irenaeus, *op. cit.*, I. 23, 5. p. 89.
24 *ibid.* I. 24, 2. p. 90.

Gnostics and Their Teachers

Basilides

Basilides was supposedly a disciple of Menander at Antioch, but he is known only from his teaching in Alexandria, where he was an active and influential Christian gnostic from *c.*120–140 AD. His extensive writings, which included a long biblical commentary, the *Exegetica*, are almost completely lost and only a few fragments survive, quoted by Clement of Alexandria. His specific doctrines are also unclear, because the patristic accounts of what Basilides taught – in the works of Irenaeus, Clement and Hippolytus – vary widely from each other. He was evidently influenced by both Christian and Platonist ideas, but his system was his own.

The cosmogonic myth of his system begins with a wholly unknowable nothingness, or 'God-who-was-Not', who 'made the cosmos from things which were not, casting down and planting a certain single seed containing within itself the whole seed-mass of the cosmos'. [25] From this emanated a series of powers, beginning with Nous (mind), who is identified with Jesus Christ, and the unfolding of a long succession of heavens: 'They [Basilides' followers] imagine that there are 365 heavens, and Abrasax is their Great Ruler, because his name comprises the cipher 365, wherefore the year consists of that number of days.' [26] It is *Abrasax* (Abraxas in Latin), the archon of the last heaven, who is the creator of the material world and thus the God of the Jews.

25 Hippolytus, *op. cit.*, 6. 21.
26 *ibid.*, 6.26

Gnosticism and Gnosis: An Introduction

Although Basilides did not teach that matter is evil, nor that marriage is wicked, salvation comes only to the elect – 'only one out of a thousand, or two out of ten thousand'[27] – by virtue of the saving knowledge of their origin and destiny. This is imparted to them by Christ, who has descended from the Pleroma in order to bring about their salvation.

But the spiritual Christ who descends is not the Jesus who is crucified: that is a mortal body occupied by the divine spirit, which ascends to the divine realm and there laughs at the archons who think they have defeated him.[28] Sin, however, is atoned for by the individual, who is forgiven for unwitting or involuntary sins, but must undergo suffering now for sins in a previous life (Basilides seems to have believed in some form of reincarnation). It is thus clear that Basilides was in no sense an antinomian, although his subsequent followers – who remained active into the fourth century – appear to have moved in that direction.

Carpocrates

Another gnostic active in Alexandria during the second century was Carpocrates, whose followers were the first to call themselves 'gnostics'. His doctrines seem to derive from Platonic thought and, like Basilides, he taught reincarnation. He rejected the Mosaic Law, and to that extent was antinomian, but it does not follow that Clement, Irenaeus and Hippolytus were justified in accusing his followers of licentious behaviour – specifically

---

27 Irenaeus, *Adversus Haereses*, I. 24, 6. The same limitation is given in *The Gospel of Thomas*, saying 23.

28 Irenaeus presents a legend that Simon of Cyrene became a substitute for Jesus on the Cross, while the real Jesus 'standing by, laughed at them.' (*Adversus Haereses*, I. 24, 4).

that they believed wives should be the common property of all – rather than seeing that Carpocrates (or perhaps his later followers) was proposing an extreme form of communal life. His creation myth is much like those of Saturnilos and Basilides, but it becomes quite distinct over the nature of Jesus:

> Carpocrates says that the cosmos and the things which are therein, came into being by the angels much below the unbegotten Father, but that Jesus was begotten by Joseph and was born like other men, though more just than the rest. And that His soul having been born strong and pure remembered what it had seen in the sphere of the unbegotten God; and that therefore a power was sent down to it from that [Father], so that by its means it might escape from the world-making angels.[29]

He is also clear as to how man is saved:

> We are saved, indeed, by means of faith and love; but all other things, while in their nature indifferent, are reckoned by the opinion of men – some good and some evil, there being nothing really evil by nature.[30]

Thus Carpocratian licentiousness, or its absence, must remain an enigma.

Marcion

Strictly speaking, Marcion should not be included here, for he was not a gnostic. But he is so often linked to them, and his doctrines do display some gnostic tendencies, that some account of him is needed – if only to show him in a true light.

---

29   Hippolytus, *op. cit.*, 6, 32.
30   Irenaeus, *op. cit.*, I. 25, 5.

Gnosticism and Gnosis: An Introduction

He was born, *c.* 85 AD, at Sinope in Pontus (now northern Turkey), where his father was a bishop, and grew up within orthodox Christianity. But he gradually developed his own views, deviating from the orthodox faith, and settled in Rome, although he kept his beliefs private until announcing them to the Roman Church in 144 AD. They were, of course, rejected and Marcion established his own church, which proved to be highly successful and a cause of great concern to the orthodox. Marcion's own writings do not survive, but from his patristic opponents we can learn the nature of his vision of Christianity.[31]

Its central theme was the absolute rejection of the God of the Old Testament, the wicked Demiurge, and with him the Jewish Law, because of his recorded cruelty and capriciousness. Matter was thus inherently evil, and against this Marcion set Christ's Gospel of Love, offered by a purely spiritual Jesus, who was sent to us in the appearance of human form by the perfect God of love and compassion. There is, however, no gnostic myth of emanation in Marcion's system: only the true Creator and the subordinate Demiurge who creates the material world, and from whom Christ has come to save us.

Marcion rejects the story of the incarnation and teaches that Christ first appeared when he began to preach at Capernaum. The crucifixion was real, but Christ only seemed to suffer. He then descended into Hell, but rescued only those who had been condemned by the Jewish God, and because matter is evil the resurrection was purely spiritual. As it will be for the saved: there can be no resurrection of the flesh.

---

31 For a full patristic analysis of Marcion, see Tertullian, *The Five Books ... against Marcion*. Translated by Peter Holmes. Edinburgh, 1868. The most accessible study of Marcion in English is still E.C. Blackman, *Marcion and His Influence*. London, 1948.

Gnostics and Their Teachers

Marcion's Christianity is thus very ascetic. The flesh is rejected so there is no marriage, no procreation and no eating of flesh. But there is equality of the sexes – because for Marcion, following Paul, in Christ there is neither male nor female – and Marcion allowed women to hold office in the church. They could baptise but, again after Paul, were forbidden to speak in church.

The emphasis on Pauline Christianity is reflected in the scriptures accepted by Marcion. It was imperative for him to set textual boundaries that enclosed his doctrines, so the Old Testament was rejected in its entirety, as were most of the Gospels. All that Marcion accepted was a truncated version of Luke's Gospel (without the birth and infancy narratives) and ten of Paul's Epistles (he excluded Timothy and Titus).

By its nature the Marcionite church could grow only by conversion, not through families, but it proved resilient, threatened the orthodox Church and survived well into the fifth century. Although his doctrines were unacceptable, even if not gnostic, Marcion's greatest effect upon the Church was to push it towards establishing a decisive Canon of Scripture, and this provided it with its greatest weapon against the gnostic systems.

Valentinus

Of all the second-century gnostics, perhaps of *all* gnostics, Valentinus was the most influential and his school the most thoroughly examined. He was born, *c.*100 AD, in lower Egypt and studied Greek philosophy in Alexandria before turning to Christianity and beginning to develop his own school. By about 140 AD he was active in Rome, where he was perceived as a heretic, and taught there for some twenty years. It is unclear whether he died there, *c.*160 AD, or in Cyprus, where Epiphanius claimed he had gone.

Valentinus was clearly well schooled in Platonic and Pythagorean philosophy and in Christian gnostic thought. His own writings were extensive, but survive certainly only in fragments quoted by Clement and Hippolytus, and possibly in the Nag Hammadi codex of *The Gospel of Truth*, which has been attributed to Valentinus or the schools deriving from him. According to Hippolytus there were two of these, the 'Italiote' (Western) and the 'Anatolic' (Eastern), differing in their view of the nature of Jesus:

> Those from Italy, whereof are Heracleon and Ptolemy [disciples of Valentinus], say that the body of Jesus was born psychic, and therefore the Spirit descended as a dove at the Baptism, that is the Word which is of the mother Sophia on high and cried aloud to the psychic man and raised him from the dead ... But those from the East, whereof are Axionicus and Bardesanes, say that the body of the Saviour was spiritual. For the Holy Spirit came upon Mary, that is Sophia and the Power of the Highest is the demiurgic art, so that that which was given by the Spirit of Mary might be moulded into form.[32]

The cosmogonic myth presented by Valentinus is more clearly Christian than are earlier forms (see p. 44 above) and also shows a Platonic influence. In summary, as set out by Irenaeus,[33] Valentinus proposed a primal duality – the Ineffable

32 Hippolytus, *op. cit.*, 6.35.
33 Irenaeus, *op. cit.*, I. 11, 1.

Gnostics and Their Teachers

and Silence – from which was emitted a second duality, called the Father and Truth. Out of these came four aeons: the Word and Life, from which ten powers were emitted; and the Human Being and the Church, which give out twelve powers. Of these one is the Mother, or Wisdom, which separated and fell from the Pleroma. Out of her were engendered the Anointed (Christ) and a shadow, from which he separated and returned to the Pleroma. Parallel to all this the Holy Spirit 'was emitted by Truth, for the scrutiny and yielding of the aeons, invisibly entering into them'.

From the shadow, which is matter, the Mother engendered the craftsman (the Demiurge) who then created the material world. The creation of man is not described by Irenaeus, but is found in one of the surviving fragments of Valentinus himself. Adam is modelled by the angels of the last aeon, on the basis of the 'pre-existent human being', and in him a 'seed of higher essence'[34] is deposited by a spiritual agency, which may be either the Word or the Mother.

Not all humans will be saved, however, for Valentinus posits the three types of man: pneumatic, psychic and hylic. The first type is destined to be saved; the second may be saved but the third is utterly lost. The distinctions between the three types are set out in detail in the words of the Valentinian Theodotus, as preserved in the *Excerpta* given by Clement of Alexandria. These excerpts also make clear that the Valentinian church's liturgical practices included baptism, chrism and the Eucharist (see p. 52 above).

---

34 Clement of Alexandria, *Stromateis*, 2.114, 3. Translated by Bentley Layton, *The Gnostic Scriptures*, p. 245. Hippolytus, *op. cit.*, 6.37.

Gnosticism and Gnosis: An Introduction

Although no complete certain works of Valentinus survive, we do have a brief hymn, and codices from Nag Hammadi that are Valentinian in content. The hymn, or psalm, is quoted by Hippolytus (who also gives an explanation):

> I behold all things hanging from air,
> I perceive all things upheld by spirit,
> Flesh hanging from soul,
> Soul standing forth from air,
> And air hanging from aether,
> But fruits borne away from Bythos
> But the embryo from the womb.[35]

Of the Valentinian texts from Nag Hammadi, *The Gospel of Truth* is generally accepted as such, while *The Gospel of Philip* and *The Tripartite Tractate* are treated with more caution. It also seems that Valentinus was influenced by *The Gospel of Thomas*, which is somewhat earlier in date. The following brief extracts from *The Gospel of Truth* will give the flavour of Valentinian Christian scripture:[36]

The proclamation of the truth is a joy for those who have received grace from the father of truth, that they might learn to know him through the power of the Word that emanated from the fullness. (I.16, 31-34) He became a way for those who

---

35 Hippolytus, *op. cit.*, 6.37.

36 *The Gospel of Truth.* Translated by Bentley Layton, *op. cit.*, pp. 253 & 259. For an exhaustive – and exhausting – survey of Valentinian thought, see Einar Thomassen, *The Spiritual Seed: The Church of the 'Valentinians'*. Leiden & Boston, 2006.

had gone astray and acquaintance for those who were without acquaintance; discovery for those who were seeking, and strength for those who were trembling; purity for those who were defiled: since it is he who is the shepherd who left behind the ninety-nine sheep that had not gone astray, and came and searched for the one that had gone astray. He rejoiced when he found it. (I. 31, 28-32, 4)

Sethians

Although no known gnostic school described itself as 'Sethian', the label was applied to some gnostic groups by Tertullian, Irenaeus, Hippolytus and Epiphanius – and it has provided scholars studying the Nag Hammadi codices with a convenient category for a variety of texts, some specifically relating to Seth (e.g. *The Gospel of the Egyptians*, *The Apocryphon of John* and *The Apocalypse of Adam*), and others in which Seth is less significant (e.g. *Three Steles of Seth*).

What these gnostics held in common was a belief that they were spiritual descendants of Seth, the third son of Adam, who was himself a saviour and a progenitor of Christ; a distinct form of cosmogonic myth (yet still similar to most gnostic forms; see above, p. 42-43) with a specific terminology; and an identification of Ialdabaoth (the Demiurge) as the specific enemy of the seed of Seth.

These Sethians, according to Hippolytus, 'are of opinion that there are three definite principles of the universals, and that each of the principles contains boundless powers' (*Philosophumena*, V. 19, 1). He then describes the intricate inter-connections between these principles and the creation of heaven and earth, and states

Gnosticism and Gnosis: An Introduction

that their ideas derive from the Orphic mysteries. More can be learned, he says, from the book *Paraphrase of Seth*, but this has not survived and we remain dependent on the relevant works of the Fathers and the various Nag Hammadi texts.[37]

The major gnostic schools of the second century, and possibly other and somewhat later schools, succeeded in surviving – and perhaps, in the case of the Valentinians, growing – within the increasingly centralised and dominant orthodox Christian Church. But by the end of the fourth century that survival had become increasingly difficult, as Christianity progressed from a tolerated religion to the official religion of the Roman Empire. Even so, the very existence of the Nag Hammadi codices demonstrates that gnostic ideas, and presumably gnostic believers, maintained a precarious foothold in the Christian world into the fifth century. During that century, however, identifiable gnostic religion effectively vanished. What precisely was it that brought this about?

---

[37] For studies of this form of gnostic thought, see Bentley Layton (Ed.), *The Rediscovery of Gnosticism*. Volume Two: Sethian Gnosticism. Leiden, 1981.

The Gnostic Diaspora: Gnosticism after Nag Hammadi

When the Emperor Theodosius decreed, in 380 AD, that Christianity, in its orthodox, catholic form, was to be the official religion of the Roman Empire, he also condemned non-Christians as 'extravagant madmen', whom he branded 'with the infamous name of Heretics'. In so doing he set in motion the gradual suppression of faiths judged to be pagan or heretical. There was, however, no widespread persecution[1] and there were none of the brutal massacres that had characterised earlier Roman persecutions of Christians.[2]

In their place came growing restrictions on the practice of pagan religion, which resulted in the steady decline of Classical Paganism. Hostility to what were perceived as Christian heresies, including heretical gnostic forms of Christianity, was even more marked and they were suppressed with increasing rigidity throughout the fifth century in both the Western and Eastern Roman Empires. Faced with official intolerance the

1 The murder of the pagan Neoplatonist philosopher Hypatia by a mob in Alexandria, in 415 AD, was an isolated incident. There was no official sanction for her death, which resulted from a false belief by the mob that she had encouraged Orestes, the pagan Prefect of Alexandria, in hostility to the Church.

2 The last and most severe persecution of Christians, under the Emperor Diocletian, took place from 303 to 311 AD. Two years later the Edict of Milan made tolerance of Christianity the official policy of the empire.

Gnosticism and Gnosis: An Introduction

Fig. 4 Nag-Hammadi in Upper Egypt

Gnosticism after Nag Hammadi

various forms of gnostic belief began to fade slowly away, but even before the Theodosian decrees came into force the process of decline had begun.

We can deduce this from the manner in which the Nag Hammadi codices had been preserved. They date from the middle of the fourth century and it is evident from scraps of papyrus in their bindings that they came from a Christian monastic library, specifically from one of the monasteries founded in the area by St. Pachomius and his successors.[3] From the care with which they sought to preserve the codices it is highly probable that the monks who copied these gnostic texts valued them and were, to some extent, sympathetic to their content, even if they were not themselves avowed gnostics. They also had good cause to hide them away.

In 367 AD St Athanasius, then Bishop of Alexandria, sent a letter to all the churches of Egypt in which he set out a definitive Canon of the Christian Scriptures[4] and identified other, non-inspired but pious texts that could be read with benefit. This was done so that innocent Christians should not 'be led astray ... and begin to pay attention to other books, the so-called apocryphal writings' – which was, presumably, what the Pachomian monks had been doing. The Apocrypha, says

3 Pachomius (*c.* 292–348 AD) converted to Christianity and took up the ascetic life after leaving the Roman army. He developed the idea of Christian coenobitic monasteries (communities of monks as opposed to solitary ascetics) and about the year 320 AD he established the first of these in Upper Egypt. At the time of his death he had eleven such monasteries under his charge and by the end of the century their number had vastly increased, including several in the neighbourhood of Chenoboskion – the present day Nag Hammadi.

4 This Canon was virtually identical with the contents of the earliest known complete biblical text, the *Codex Sinaiticus*, that was produced in the mid-fourth century. It is now in the British Library.

Gnosticism and Gnosis: An Introduction

Athanasius, 'are a fabrication of the heretics, who write them down when it pleases them and generously assign to them an early date of composition' so that they can claim them 'as supposedly ancient writings' and thus 'deceive the guileless'.[5] Athanasius may not have been a tolerant man, but he was certainly perceptive – and successful in establishing what became an almost universally adopted Canon of Scripture.

But official condemnation of gnostic texts and intolerance of gnostic belief systems were not in themselves enough to bring an end to Gnosticism. Other factors were also at work.

Triumph and defeat

Early Christianity was not a monolithic structure. The Christian faith was understood, expressed and practised in a great variety of ways, but by the end of the fourth century what may be termed orthodox, catholic Christianity was the dominant form, accepted by the vast majority of professing Christians. There was still dissent and there were still gnostic Christians, but the triumph of orthodoxy was a fact. And we should not lose sight of that fact if we choose to speculate on what might have been had some form of gnostic Christianity become the basis of the established faith. If we ask the question, 'what was the appeal of gnostic beliefs?', we must also consider just *why* gnostic beliefs failed to capture the popular mind and heart. One argument advanced to explain its appeal is that,

> Gnosticism had powerful attractions in the second century, notably for Christians of moderate or

[5] Athanasius, 39th Festal Letter for the year 367, in W. Schneemelcher (Ed.), *New Testament Apocrypha*. Cambridge, 1991. Vol. 1, pp. 49-50. English translation ed. by R.McL. Wilson.

mediocre education who were troubled by the more sub-Christian parts of the Old Testament and repelled by the crudity of uninstructed believers.

And as a consequence,

Reaction to Gnosticism led simple believers to make strident denials that baptismal faith required any supplementation and correction by higher and more philosophic knowledge.[6]

Nor were 'simple believers' alone in this attitude: both Tertullian and Hippolytus looked upon philosophy – especially Greek philosophy – as a source of heresy. More reflective Christian scholars, such as Clement and Origen, saw the merit of true 'gnosis' and recognised that faith and knowledge were not mutually exclusive but necessary complements to one another.

In this they differed also from the gnostic attitude, which may be seen, in some respects, as a mirror image of 'simple' Christian believers: knowledge rather than faith being the key to salvation. And such knowledge was not perceived in an abstract sense, as something to be acquired for its own sake; it was much more the infallible means to spiritual attainment, to the direct experience of God that has always been the goal of the mystic. Except that mystics did not find the way of ascent to God through secret knowledge, intellectual or otherwise. The way for the mystic is the path of disciplined contemplation and surrender to Divine Grace, not that of overcoming hostile spiritual beings by words and signs of power.

6 Henry Chadwick, 'The Beginning of Christian Philosophy', in A.H. Armstrong (Ed.), *The Cambridge History of Later Greek and Early Medieval Philosophy*. Cambridge, 1970, Ch. 9, p. 165.

Gnosticism and Gnosis: An Introduction

It would be unjust to dismiss all gnostic spirituality as mechanical and self-seeking. There are passages of undeniable poetic beauty and spiritual insight in many gnostic texts and a constant underlying yearning for a return to a primal, unsullied spiritual state. But this is also the goal for orthodox Christians, and those who sought to attain it by following the ascetic path of renunciation were catered for by the monastic movement that grew rapidly from the fourth century onwards. And this way was, of course, open to any and all Christians who felt its call and could accept its rigours. Gnosticism, on the other hand, was decidedly elitist and thus, by its very nature, could never hold the mass appeal of the orthodox Church.

We do not know the precise numbers of believers in specific gnostic systems in the various provinces of the Roman Empire, but there are approximate figures for adherents of different religions in the city of Rome. The historian of religion, Hubert Cancik, estimated that in second-century Rome – which had a population of about one million – there were between 50,000 and 80,000 Jews; 20,000 to 30,000 followers of Egyptian cults (and a similar number for Syrian cults); about 20,000 Christians, and some 10,000 adherents of Mithraism. By comparison, the estimated figure for gnostics is minuscule: no more than a few hundred.[7]

It is probable that in Egypt, especially around Alexandria, and in Asia Minor, the number of gnostics at this period was greater, but even with a broad definition of Gnosticism it is unlikely that gnostic beliefs posed a numerical threat to orthodox

---

[7] These figures are given in I.P. Couliano, *The Tree of Gnosis*, San Francisco, 1992, p. 30, citing H. Cancik, 'Gnostiker in Rom', in J. Taubes (Ed.), *Gnosis und Politik*, Munich, 1984, p. 172.

Gnosticism after Nag Hammadi

Christianity. However, they continued to attract the hostility of the Church Fathers and, eventually, of the state. The response of gnostic teachers – not all of whom, it should be noted, were or professed to be Christian – seems to have been to move, with their followers, to the margins of the Eastern Empire and into lands beyond the control of Rome. There they survived and, in some of their well-established forms, thrived, well beyond the fourth century. Not all were strictly gnostic, but those that derived from Jewish–Christian sources were unquestionably heterodox.

Gnosticism in the East

We know from Hippolytus and Irenaeus, and from the Nag Hammadi texts, that various Christian and Jewish gnostic sects engaged in ritual bathing and immersion, for reasons of either purification or initiation.[8] Within orthodox circles baptism was, of course, the crucial element of Christian initiation, and ritual bathing was important within Judaism – notably among the Essenes. There were also heterodox Jewish sects that emphasised baptism in their ritual practices and also displayed gnostic elements in their belief systems. Among these were the Elkesaites, a second-century movement that originated in Mesopotamia and was influential in preserving gnostic beliefs among the heterodox groups that descended, directly or indirectly, from them.

---

8   See, *e.g.*, Hippolytus, on the Naassenes (*Philosophumena*, V, 7): 'For the promise of baptism is not anything else ... than the leading to unfading pleasure him who is baptised ... in living water' (Vol. 1, p. 125). There is also an account of gnostic baptism in *The Gospel of Philip* (72-75), *The Nag Hammadi Scriptures*, pp. 176-179.

Gnosticism and Gnosis: An Introduction

Nothing is known of Elchasai, the supposed founder of the Elkesaites, other than what is reported by Hippolytus. According to his account, one Alcibiades of Apamea, in Syria, arrived in Rome, about 120 AD, bringing a book containing the teaching of Elchasai as revealed to him by a gigantic angel.[9] The angel, said to be the Son of God, was accompanied by a female, of similarly vast form, 'who is called the Holy Spirit'.

Through this book 'a new remission of sins was brought as good news to men', especially to those who were sexual sinners. Such a sinner should, 'immediately he hears this book' be re-baptised – by full immersion while fully clothed – 'in the name of the Great and Highest God and in the name of His Son, the Great King'. While doing this, the penitent should

> call to witness the seven witnesses who are written in this book, the Heaven and the Water, and the Holy Spirit and the Angel of Prayer and the oil and the salt and the Earth.[10]

The Elkesaites did not treat Christ as divine, but as a man who had been born and reborn many times, 'alternating births and changing one body for another'. They were also involved in occultism and magic, believing that they could foretell the future, while they

> give heed to mathematics and astrology and magic as if they were true, and they use these things to astonish the weak-minded, so that they may think

---

9 The angel was said to have been 96 miles tall, with a girth of 16 miles, a shoulder breadth of 24 miles, and footprints 14 miles long! (Hippolytus, *op. cit.*, IX.3.13, Vol. 2, p. 133).

10 Hippolytus, *op. cit.*, IX.3.15, Vol. 2, p. 135.

Gnosticism after Nag Hammadi

themselves partakers in a mighty matter. They give also incantations and spells to those bitten by dogs and to possessed and other diseased persons.[11]

It is not these supposed magical activities, however, that distinguish the Elkesaites and their descendants among similar heterodox groups. Their significance is twofold. It lies in the continuation of their practices by the Nasoreans – who survive today as the Mandaeans, which name means 'gnostics' – and in their rejection by Mani, the founder and prophet of the only gnostic world religion, and the most influential gnostic of all. But before we take up the story of the Mandaeans and the Manichees there is a brief digression to be made, to the ideas of Bardaisan of Edessa, in Syria, a teacher who has been described as 'the last of the Gnostics'.[12]

The description is debatable, for although his opponents claimed that Bardaisan (c.154–222 AD) was a disciple of Valentinus, there are no clearly gnostic or dualist concepts in his surviving works: *The Book of the Laws of Countries (The Dialogue of Fate)* and a collection of hymns. He was, however, a syncretist who had been strongly influenced by Chaldean astrology – which he later rejected – and who tried to fit Christianity into a mould that would satisfy the Judaeo-Christian, Greek and Iranian traditions alike.

Bardaisan departed from orthodoxy in a variety of ways. He denied that there was any material resurrection, either for Christ or for mankind, and he taught a vaguely gnostic cosmology in which, according to his opponents,

11   *idem*. IX.3.14, Vol. 2, p. 135.

12   This was the sub-title of a book on Bardaisan by the German theologian, Adolf Hilgenfeld. See H.J.W.Drijvers, *Bardaisan of Edessa*. Assen, 1966, p. 8.

> this world .... is composed of Five Entities, viz. Fire and Wind and Water and Light and Darkness. Each of these was standing in its own region, Light in the East, Wind in the West, Fire in the South, Water in the North, the Lord of them all in the Height, and their Enemy, the Dark, in the Depth below.[13]

Inevitably, there was confusion among the entities and the Dark threatened to overwhelm them, but they called upon God, and 'the Word' (Christ) 'came down and cut off the Dark from being in the midst of the pure Entities, and it was hurled down and fell to the lower part of its nature'. It was also claimed that his followers – and thus Bardaisan himself – believed in

> a Good and an Evil (God) and [they] teach fortunate constellations and destinies, like the Manichaeans. They proclaim the Seven and the Twelve, deprive the Creator of the power of ruling the world, deny the freedom of man and vilify the resurrection of the bodies, like the Marcionites and the Manichaeans. They wear and wrap themselves in white clothing, because they say that who wears white clothes belongs to the followers of Good, and who wears black, to the followers of Evil.[14]

Ultimately Bardaisan was forced by the Church to leave Edessa, but despite the claims made about his doctrines they were not like those of Mani, nor do they resemble those of

---

13 Moses bar Kepha, a ninth century Syrian theologian, quoted in C.W. Mitchell (Trans.), S. Ephraim's *Prose Refutations of Mani, Marcion, and Bardaisan*. Completed by A.A. Bevan and F.C. Burkitt. London, 1921. Vol. II, p. cxxii.

14 From the heretical catalogue of the fourth century Syrian theologian, Maruta of Maipherkat. See Drijvers, *op. cit.*, pp. 106-107.

Gnosticism after Nag Hammadi

the Mandaeans, for all that their faith has always laid great emphasis on ritual baptism.

Exclusive Gnosticism and missionary gnosis

Mandaeans

The Mandaeans, or Nasoreans as they were in the second century, have survived persecution and dispersal for almost two millennia, and they are the only living community that can truly be described as gnostic. They originated as a Jewish–Christian (or possibly pre-Christian) baptising sect that left Palestine to settle in Mesopotamia; by their own accounts the Mandaeans came from Haran, which is close to Edessa. They also settled further east in Iran, where they suffered under Zoroastrian rule and later endured periodical persecution after the rise of Islam. In recent years the Mandaeans have been largely driven from their homelands and survive as communities in exile in the Middle East and further afield.[15]

Their religion is without question gnostic, but with emphases and features that are unique to the Mandaeans. The very name derives from their word *manda*, meaning knowledge or gnosis, which identifies them as 'the knowing ones', or gnostics, although it is strictly only the laity who are 'Mandaeans'. What is most important for them are the ritual practices, especially those surrounding the threefold immersion in flowing water

---

15 During the 1990s many of the *c.* 60,000 strong Mandaean community in Iraq fled to Syria and Jordan when the Marshlands where they lived were destroyed. After the Iraq War of 2003 they suffered further persecution from Islamists in both Iraq and Iran, and only a few thousand remain in those two countries.

Gnosticism and Gnosis: An Introduction

that ensures spiritual purity. Those who enter the priesthood and strictly follow the rules of ritual purity are termed *tarmidi*, while the few who go on to gain a true understanding of the secret doctrines, and thus achieve enlightenment, are termed Nasoraeans.

Unlike the practices of ancient gnostic systems, those of the Mandaeans have been observed at first hand and recorded in great detail. Similarly, Mandaean literature, which almost certainly predates the rise of Islam, has been preserved, copied and passed down for many centuries. Much of it has been made available – sometimes against the wishes of the Mandaeans themselves – as texts and translations over the course of the last century.

The most important work is the *Ginza*, the Great Book or Treasure, which is in two parts. The 'Right Ginza' is concerned with cosmology and doctrinal speculation, and contains also a code of moral law, while the 'Left Ginza' deals with the soul's salvation: its way of ascent to the realm of light. There is also a significant liturgical collection, known in translation as *The Canonical Prayer Book*,[16] that contains hymns and prayers together with details of rites and ceremonies still in use. Other texts include the *Haran Gawaita*, which although incomplete is a valuable source for early Mandaean history.

The Mandaean cosmogony is typically gnostic, with a clear division of the world of light from the world of darkness. The light world is the creation of the 'First Life', or 'King of

---

16   *The Canonical Prayer Book of the Mandaeans*: Text, notes and translation by E.S. Drower. Leiden, 1959. There is no full English translation of the *Ginza*, but extracts are printed in Foerster, *op. cit.*, Vol. 2.

Gnosticism after Nag Hammadi

Light', from whom descend an expanding series of emanations. Below and against this world is the Darkness, whose ruler is responsible – by way of the Demiurge, *Pthahil* – for the creation of the material world and of humanity. But,

> darkness and light are bound together: had there been no dark then light would not have come into being. The worlds of darkness and light are Body and counterpart: they complement one another. Neither can remove from or approach the other.[17]

Indeed,

> betwixt darkness and light there can be no union or pact: on the contrary, hatred enmity and dissension, …. For darkness is the adversary of light. They are Right and Left, they are *ruha* [vital spirit] and *nisimta* [soul]; moreover they are called Adam and Eve.[18]

Yet Adam has a spark of light (the Hidden Adam) that can and must be saved through the work of a series of mythological saviours or messengers, including Adam's immediate descendants.

There are also prophets, such as John the Baptist, who is revered by the Mandaeans for opposing Jesus Christ – seen through their eyes as an apostate and liar. John is the ideal baptiser, whose role is carried on by the Mandaean priests. The sanctuary (*manda*), where the purificatory rites – immersion, sealing, anointing, the laying on of hands and communion – are

---

17 *Alf Trisar Suialia*. trans. E.S. Drower. Berlin, 1960, pp. 134 & 213. Quoted in Drower, *The Secret Adam: A Study of Nasoraean Gnosis*. Oxford, 1960. p. 5.

18 *ibid*. p. 145. (p. 6)

carried out, is set within an enclosure that must include a ritual pool of flowing water which is called the 'Jordan': a memory of the legendary origin of these baptismal practices.

The complexities of Mandaean doctrines and cosmology are too involved to be set out here in more detail than the brief outline given above, but it should be emphasised that for the Mandaeans salvation comes by means of a complex interweaving of saving knowledge and ritual observance: effectively gnosis in both theory and practice. Their religion is, because of its derivation from baptising sects, atypical of classical gnostic systems but because it is a living and practising faith, its study has greatly enriched our understanding of gnostic religion.[19]

Mani and Manichaeism

A baptising sect was also the source, albeit by way of rejection, of the Manichaean religion. Mani, the prophet of that religion, was born in 216 AD near Seleucia-Ctesiphon on the Tigris, and grew up among the Elkesaites to whom his father had been drawn and from whom Mani derived his asceticism.

At the age of twelve Mani had a visionary experience of his 'Heavenly Twin', whom he later identified, after a further experience when he was twenty-four, as the Holy Spirit. During this second visionary episode Mani received a series of dramatic revelations:

19 It is unfortunate that the most important research into the Mandaeans, by Kurt Rudolph, has not been translated into English, but the studies and translations of E.S. [Lady] Drower, who lived and worked among the Mandaeans of Iraq are also valuable (see, *e.g.*, *The Mandaeans of Iraq and Iran, their Cults, Customs, Magic, Legends, and Folklore.* Oxford, 1937). Her work is complemented by a more recent, and very accessible study of Edmondo Lupieri, *The Mandaeans: The Last Gnostics.* Grand Rapids, 2002.

Gnosticism after Nag Hammadi

> The Living Paraclete came down to me and spoke to me. he revealed to me the hidden mystery that was hidden from the worlds and the generations: the mystery of the Depth and the Height: he revealed to me the mystery of the Light and the Darkness, the mystery of the conflict and the great war which the Darkness stirred up. .... He instructed me on the mystery of the Tree of Knowledge of which Adam ate, by which his eyes were made to see. .... Thus was revealed to me by the Paraclete all that has been and that shall be, ... Through him I learned to know every thing, I saw the All through him, and I became one body and one spirit.[20]

After this Mani knew that he was truly an apostle of Jesus:

> He wrote [thus again and] said in the Gospel of his most holy hope: 'I, Mani, an apostle of Jesus Christ through the will of God, the Father of Truth, from whom I also was born, who lives and abides forever, existing before all and also abiding after all.'[21]

But Mani failed to convince the Elkesaites of who he was and they – apart from his father and two disciples – rejected both him and his doctrines. He then began his missionary career, initially within Persia but soon after in the Indus valley. When he returned, some two years later, he was well received by the new king, Shapur I, who accepted Mani's new religion and it began to take root and spread. Missionaries carried his doctrines

---

20 *Kephalaia (Chapters)* From I, 14:29-15.24. Quoted in Hans Jonas, *The Gnostic Religion*. Second edition, revised. Boston, 1963, pp. 208-209.

21 *Cologne Mani Codex* 65.20 – 66.11. (Quoted in Majella Franzmann, *Jesus in the Manichaean Writings*. London, 2003, p. 15.)

and practices across the Persian Empire and beyond: eastward along the Silk Road to Central Asia and China, and westward into the Roman Empire, where they made both converts and enemies.

Fig. 5 Mani

But a later king, Bahram I, upheld the old Zoroastrian religion and in 276 AD Mani was arrested and executed, probably by crucifixion, although the term may serve simply to emphasise his martyrdom as a parallel to the death of Jesus. His church, however, lived on.

Manichaean missionaries established churches in Syria, in Egypt and in the provinces around the Mediterranean, in both Europe and North Africa, and it grew numerically and in influence to a degree that alarmed the orthodox Christian Churches. Ultimately the Manichaean religion faded in the West, because it faced not only the hostility of the Church but also persecution from the state: in 297 AD, the Emperor Diocletian outlawed Manichaeism, which he identified – rightly – as essentially Persian, and thus representative of Rome's greatest enemy. When Christianity became the official religion of Rome the Manichees could have no significant future within the empire. They also had no major thinkers to promote their faith, and could never win intellectual arguments with such men as Augustine, the greatest Christian theologian of his era, who had a thorough understanding of their faith because he had himself been a Manichee in his youth. Hostility to Manichaeism was also intensified because it was perceived as a faith that posed a greater threat to the Church than other gnostic systems, because Manichaeism, like orthodox Christianity, offered itself to all, not to just an elite few.

One result of this is that we possess a significant number of anti-Manichaean texts,[22] together with many works attributed to Mani, and others by his followers. These Manichaean texts came to light through a series of fortunate discoveries that parallel the Nag Hammadi finds, and it is necessary to set them out in some detail as they also illustrate the extent and history of the Manichaean religion.

The first discoveries were made in Chinese Central Asia during the early years of the twentieth century. These consisted of some thousands of textual fragments, in various Central Asian

---

22 Among the most important are those of St Augustine (e.g. *Contra Faustum; Contra Fortunatum*; and *De Haeresibus*); Ephraem Syrus (*Prose Refutations*); and Theodore bar Koni (*Book of Scholia*).

Gnosticism and Gnosis: An Introduction

languages, from Turfan; and more substantial Manichaean manuscripts in Chinese, from Dunhuang. In 1918, a partial Manichaean codex in Latin was found in Algeria, followed by a series of finds in Egypt. The first of these consisted of fragments in Syriac, and then, in 1929, came the discovery, at Medinet Madi, of a series of very early Manichaean texts in Coptic. Some of these were lost during World War Two, but the *Kephalaia*, the *Homilies* and the *Psalm Book* have been published. Even more significant is a fifth-century codex in Greek, known as the *Cologne Mani Codex*, that was found at Assiut in Egypt in the late 1960s. The most recent discoveries have been made at Kellis in Upper Egypt, where large numbers of textual fragments in Greek, Coptic and Syriac have been found in continuing excavations that began in 1991.

From all of this it has been possible to piece together a coherent picture of Manichaean life and thought, although Mani's cosmography and cosmogony are extremely complex – far more so than any earlier gnostic system – and it is impossible to do them justice in a limited space. What follows is thus necessarily simplified and condensed.[23]

Mani's system

Mani's cosmos represents his absolute dualism: there are two eternal, uncreated substances in perpetual opposition. They are Truth/Light, the essence of 'God', and 'Matter', which is

---

[23] Longer and more detailed, but accessible, accounts of Mani's cosmogony and doctrines are to be found in Jonas, *op. cit.*, pp. 209-236, and in H.J. Klimkeit, *Gnosis on the Silk Road: Gnostic Texts from Central Asia*. San Francisco, 1993, pp. 4-20. There is also an English translation of Theodore bar Koni's 'On Mani's Teachings concerning the Beginning of the World' in A.V. Williams-Jackson, *Researches in Manichaeism*. New York, 1932, pp. 221-254.

Gnosticism after Nag Hammadi

Darkness and deceit – everlasting, irredeemable evil. Light, harmonious and whole, seeks to remain eternally separate; it does not strive to illuminate or redeem Darkness. But the divided, self-destructive Darkness expanded beyond its boundary, became aware of the Light and sought to absorb it.

This initiated a reaction in the Light, but the Light could not respond in kind to anything evil, and so called into being a 'Primal Man', sometimes presented as 'Soul', which was the beginning of a progression of successive emanations. Primal Man was at first defeated and consumed by Darkness, but in this absorption of a part of Light the Darkness begins its own weakening, for the Primal Man has effectively poisoned the Darkness.

Then follow successive creations of the Light. First, Living Spirit, who separates the admixture of Light and Dark from the absolute Darkness and sets in motion the process of release or salvation, followed by a progressive creation of the macrocosm. Next, the 'Third Creation' of Light produces a Messenger and the powers who support him, who engage in a continuing struggle with the aggressive Darkness. Then animal and plant life appear on the Earth, to be followed by the first man and woman. But the flesh is contaminated with evil; Adam is weak and is seduced by Eve, and through procreation the imprisonment of light is perpetuated.

But each material human being contains a fragment of light, which must be drawn out and returned to the Light, and this requires the coming of a saviour. So the Messenger finally emanates the luminous Jesus, who both reveals truth and saves man through his apparent suffering on the cross:

Gnosticism and Gnosis: An Introduction

> I bore these things until I had fulfilled the will of my Father; the First Man is my Father whose will I have carried out.
>
> Lo, the Darkness I have subdued; lo, the fire of the fountains I have extinguished, as the Sphere turns hurrying round, as the sun receives the refined part of life.
>
> O soul, rise thy eyes to the height and contemplate thy bond ... lo, thy fathers are calling thee.
>
> Now go aboard the Ship of Light and receive thy garland of glory and return to thy kingdom and rejoice with all the Aeons.[24]

However, to complete the work of our salvation from evil – from Matter, from Darkness – a series of saviour figures is needed, from the primal, 'luminous' Jesus down to Mani, by way of Buddha, Zoroaster and the historical Jesus. It is also essential for us not only to know the truth, but to live in the right manner, which requires no small degree of renunciation and asceticism. Mani recognised that not all of his followers were able to achieve this, and so divided them into two categories: the Elect, or the Righteous, and the Hearers – analogous to the Faithful and the Catechumens of the early Christian Church. Only the Elect, whose code of conduct was much more strict, were certain of salvation, but hearers could attain to the status of the Elect when they were ready to accept the rigorous asceticism required.

---

24 *Manichaean Psalm Book*, Psalm 246, 55. Quoted in Jonas, *op. cit.*, pp. 229-230

Gnosticism after Nag Hammadi

Manichaeism in practice

Despite opposition, hostility and the ever-present threat of persecution,[25] Manichaeism expanded across Central Asia and maintained its presence in the near East, North Africa and the edges of the Byzantine Empire. Its success was due partly to its openness in accepting converts, and partly to Mani's readiness to absorb appropriate elements from other religions – principally from Christianity and Zoroastrianism, but also from Buddhism – and Manichaeism developed into a world religion: the only one of a gnostic type to attain such a status. It is also the only gnostic religion for which there are substantial surviving manuscripts that illustrate its structure and practices as well as its doctrines.

As Manichaeism grew, so did the need for an efficient organisation that would maintain the ordered structure of the Manichaean church and preserve its doctrinal purity. This took a strictly hierarchical form, with Mani himself as the active head of his church. After his death the church was directed by his deputy (Addai), and his successors, who had the title of archegos (prince, or chief). Below the archegos, in descending order, were twelve apostles, or teachers; seventy-two bishops; and 360 priests. The dedicated believers, both men and women, formed the Elect and the more casual adherents of the church constituted the Hearers (auditores).

---

25 Persecution of the Manichees was not confined to Eastern or Western Christianity. The rise of Islam led to increasingly frequent attacks within the Muslim Caliphates, and within and around the Chinese Empire both Buddhists and Confucians were decidedly hostile – as was the state itself.

Gnosticism and Gnosis: An Introduction

Believers received doctrinal instruction – salvation required that they know the truth – but what was more important was the practice of Manichaeism. There were strict rules for each group, which, if broken, required confession and penance. The behaviour of the Elect was summarised in 'Three Seals' and 'Five Commandments', while for the Hearers there were 'Ten Commandments'. The seals, restricted to the Elect, were those of the mouth (to abstain from eating meat and drinking wine); of the hand (to avoid injuring any living thing, or water, or fire); and of the breast (to maintain sexual purity and not to marry).

The Five Commandments of the Elect were: Not to lie; Not to injure; To remain chaste; Not to eat meat or drink wine; and To embrace poverty so as not to covet. There is no complete list of the Hearers' Ten Commandments, but they appear to have been an extended list of prohibitions although not as restrictive as those for the Elect (*e.g.* they were to renounce adultery but were not forbidden to marry).

Manichaean ritual practices were closely related to the rules for life. Thus there was a daily sacred meal, which utilised the bread and fruit brought to the Elect as offerings from the Hearers. Some days were reserved for fasting and during the year there were five night festivals and the annual festival of the Bema, which was the most important Manichean celebration. The Bema commemorated Mani's martyrdom and ascent to heaven, where he would sit in judgement until the end of time when Jesus would take his place on the judgement seat (the Bema). In the ceremony an empty seat symbolised Mani's spiritual presence.

Gnosticism after Nag Hammadi

There were also scriptural readings, for although the Manichees rejected the Old Testament they did accept parts of the New Testament, especially some of the Epistles, together with ritual prayers, hymns and psalms. Many of these have been preserved and a few verses will serve to illustrate their nature:

> 1   Let us worship the spirit of the Paraclete.
>
> 2   Let us bless our Lord Jesus who sent to us the Spirit of Truth. He came; he separated us from the error of the world. He brought us a mirror. We looked; we saw this universe in it.
>
> [And at the end of time]
>
> 19   A new aeon will be built in the place of this world which will be destroyed, so that in it the powers of the Light may reign, because they have done, they have fulfilled the entire will of the Father. They have subdued the hated one; they have [power?] over him forever.
>
> 21   Glory and victory to our Lord Manichaios, the Spirit of [Truth] who is from the Father, the one who revealed to us the beginning, the middle and the end. Victory to the soul of the [blessed] Mary, Theona, Pshaijmnoute.[26]

And yet, despite the energy of Manichaean missionaries, and their undoubted success over the course of a thousand year, and for all the evident appeal of Mani's creed, Manichaeism

---

26   *Coptic Manichaean Psalm-Book*. Psalm 223: Verses from a Bema Psalm. In J.D. BeDuhn, 'Manichaean Theology', in Richard Valantasis (Ed.), *Religions of Antiquity in Practice*. Princeton, 2000, pp. 481-483.

Gnosticism and Gnosis: An Introduction

finally failed. Continuing hostility from the Christian Church, increasing persecution within Islamic states, and the waves of conquest and political change that swept over Central and Eastern Asia, gradually eroded the influence and very existence of the Manichaean church. In the West it remained active only on the fringes of the Byzantine Empire, from where it inspired, directly and indirectly, new dualist variations of Christianity. These flourished where and when they could, but none of them survived. A verse from the Manichaean Hymn about the Captivity of Light supplies them with a suitable epitaph:

> Lo, that great Kingdom of Salvation [waits] on high, Ready for those who have gnosis, so that they may finally find peace.[27]

To complete the story of Gnosticism, however, the most significant of these Manichaean offshoots – if they can legitimately be so called – must be presented in outline.

Paulicians and Bogomils

From the fall of the Western Roman Empire in the fifth-century to the final defeat of the Byzantine Empire by Muslim Turks in 1453, the Orthodox Greek Church successfully resisted and overcame both its internal schisms and the various heretical movements that periodically challenged its religious supremacy. Very few of these movements were clearly and overtly dualist in nature, and it is uncertain if any of them derived directly from Manichaeism or other gnostic sources. Two of them, however, were certainly claimed by their opponents to have been infected

---

[27] Hans-Joachim Klimkeit (Trans.), *Gnosis on the Silk Road: Gnostic Texts from Central Asia*. San Francisco, 1993, p. 38.

Gnosticism after Nag Hammadi

with Mani's doctrines. These were the Paulicians, who first appeared in the late seventh-century, and the later Bogomils, who seem to have derived from the former and were well established on the borders of the empire by the tenth century.

The Paulicians were established in Armenia by Constantine of Mananali, a former Manichaean who sought to remodel his faith in a more Christian form. Taking the name of Silvanus (Silas), one of the companions of St. Paul, he rejected Manichaean texts and required his followers to use only the New Testament – although he provided a dualistic interpretation of the Scriptures 'to those few among them whom they know to be more perfect in impiety' and among whom 'the heresy of the Manichaeans is observed and honoured ... in deep silence'.[28]

They denied that Christ took on a bodily form and looked upon the material world as the creation of an evil demiurge. The Paulicians were not absolute dualists, however, but seem to have followed classic gnostic ideas, which they were said to have adopted from the works of Basilides. Their beliefs about matter do not seem to have affected their concerns with this world, and they developed into an aggressive military power, which seems to have been as much a cause of, as a reaction to, their continuing, if intermittent, persecution by the Byzantines.

The greatest Paulician success was achieved in the early ninth century, when the Paulician leader Sergius – who called himself Tychicus, after another of St Paul's followers – revived the faith, and by his personal charisma and missionary zeal expanded its activity so that there were seven distinct Paulician

---

28 Peter of Sicily, *Historia Manichaeorum*, Col. 1252. Quoted in D. Obolensky, *The Bogomils: A Study in Balkan Neo-Manichaeism*. Cambridge, 1948, p. 33.

Gnosticism and Gnosis: An Introduction

'churches' throughout Armenia and Asia Minor. In the decades following his death Paulician political power reached its zenith, but after the defeat of their military leader, Chrysochir, in 872 AD, they entered a long decline. Paulician communities, some in name only, survived in Armenia and other frontier areas of the Empire throughout the Middle Ages, and down to the nineteenth century. These late survivals, however, bore no resemblance to their putative Manichaean forebears.

The Bogomils

The second great 'Manichaean' heresy arose in the tenth century, beyond the borders of Byzantium in the Kingdom of Bulgaria. This movement originated with a priest, Bogomil (*i.e.* beloved of God), about whom nothing is known save his name. It probably developed within Paulician communities, as it displayed features in common with, or closely resembling, the earlier heresy. The Bogomils were dualist, and although much of what we know of their doctrines comes from the writings of their enemies, these seem to have painted an accurate picture. Thus, in the late tenth century Cosmas, a Bulgarian Orthodox priest, wrote, in his Sermon against the Heretics, that the Bogomils stated, 'We reject David and the prophets. We admit only the gospel; we do not carry out our lives according to the law of Moses, but according to the law given through the apostles.' Cosmas also condemned the Bogomils for their rejection of the Trinity, the Mass, the Mosaic Law and the prophets, and their opposition to marriage and meat-eating.[29]

29 See Edward Peters (Ed.), *Heresy and Authority in Medieval Europe: Documents in Translation*. London, 1980, p. 112.

Gnosticism after Nag Hammadi

There is also a surviving Latin translation of the *Book of John the Evangelist* (an early Bogomil text also known as the *Secret Book*), which was brought, in the thirteenth century, from Bulgaria to Northern Italy by Nazarius, a Bogomil bishop. Nazarius was examined by Rainier Sacconi, an inquisitor who had earlier been a dualist Paterene, and professed beliefs that mirror those in the book. This *Secret Book* sets out Bogomil cosmogony in detail, as these examples illustrate:

> And I [John] said: Lord, before Satan fell, in what glory abode he with thy Father? And he said unto me: In such glory was he that he commanded the powers of the heavens: but I sat with my Father, and he did order all the followers of the Father, and went down from heaven unto the deep and ascended up out of the deep unto the throne of the invisible Father. And he saw the glory of him that moveth the heavens, and he thought to set his seat above the clouds of heaven and desired to be like unto the Most High.
>
> And he devised furthermore and made man in his likeness, and commanded the angel of the third heaven to enter into the body of clay. And he took thereof and made another body in the form of a woman, and commanded the angel of the second heaven to enter into the body of the woman. But the angel lamented when they beheld a mortal shape upon them and that they were unlike in shape. And he commanded them to do the deed of the flesh in the bodies of clay, and they knew not how to commit sin.

Gnosticism and Gnosis: An Introduction

> And after that I, John, asked of the Lord, saying: How say men that Adam and Eve were created by God and set in paradise to keep the commandments of the Father, and were delivered unto death? And the Lord said to me: Hearken, John, beloved of my Father; foolish men say thus in their deceitfulness that my Father made bodies of clay: but by the Holy Ghost made he all the powers of the heavens, and holy ones were found having bodies of clay because of their transgression, and therefore were delivered unto death.[30]

Bogomil doctrines were evidently gnostic in tone and substance, although they derive only indirectly – via Mani and the Paulicians – from the gnostics of the early centuries. Their practices also echo those of the Manichaeans. There was a hierarchy but the sacraments of the orthodox Church were rejected: baptism was by the Holy Spirit, and as they did not believe in a material Jesus, the Eucharist had no meaning. Bogomil missionaries were more concerned to preach what they believed to be the pure Christianity of the New Testament, and there was never a Bogomil political entity nor military aggression. It was thus as heretics that the Bogomils were persecuted.

Even so, the Bogomil faith spread throughout the Balkans – especially within Serbia – into Greece and other parts of the Byzantine Empire, and its missionaries were active and successful in Italy and elsewhere in Western Europe. With the fall of Constantinople and the spread of Islam across South-Eastern Europe, Bogomilism declined and eventually died out. But in its earlier, proselytising period it stimulated the last

---

30 The English translation is given in M.R. James, *The Apocryphal New Testament... Newly translated.* Oxford, 1924, pp. 188, 189 & 190.

Gnosticism after Nag Hammadi

upsurge of dualist religion in Europe, and the greatest spiritual threat to catholic Christianity since the days of Mani.

Mediaeval dualism in Europe: the Cathars

When he wrote his book against the heretics, Irenaeus, then Bishop of Lyons, was concerned with gnostics active in his city. Almost one thousand years later there was another irruption of dualist heresy – identified as Manichaean, and thus as gnostic – in Southern France. The reasons for this late upsurge of dualism are complex, but it was fuelled partly by post-millennial fears, by the uncertainties of social change and by a pervasive religious flux due, in turn, to a revulsion at the perceived hypocrisy of a corrupt priesthood concerned with temporal power rather than with spirituality and moral integrity.

Missionaries of the Bogomils and other dualist sects (*e.g.* the Paterini in Lombardy) had been active in Western Europe from the eleventh century onwards and in 1163, at the Council of Tours, the generic name of 'Cathars' (from the Greek καθαρός, *katharos*, 'pure') was applied to them. They caused alarm within the Church across Europe, but especially in the Languedoc, in South-Western France, where social and political conditions ensured their wide acceptance.[31] Because they were centred on Albi, where a great debate between Catholics and Cathars was held in 1165, they were known to their opponents as Albigenses.

---

31 There were significant Cathar communities in Italy. Rainier Sacconi, (*Of the Sects of Modern Heretics.* 1254; see Maitland, *Facts and Documents*, pp. 427-428), gives these numbers for Cathar churches in Italy in the mid-thirteenth century: Verona and other Lombard cities: *c.*500, of both sexes; Contorezo: 1,500+; Bagnolenses: Mantua, Brescia, Bergamo etc. *c.* 200; and Trevisano: *c.*150.

Gnosticism and Gnosis: An Introduction

Ten years after this a council of dualist believers was held at St Felix de Caraman, under the direction of Nicetas, the Bogomil Bishop of Constantinople, and an identifiable Cathar church was established. Three bishops were appointed, for major cities in the Cathar heartland: Toulouse, Carcassonne and Albi, and the Cathar church flourished in its season – which proved to be short-lived. Its chequered history and the reasons for its initial triumph and ultimate destruction must be given briefly, and only in the barest outline, but first we must consider the nature of Catharism.

The Cathars were unquestionably dualist and, in the eyes of their opponents, they were Manichaean heretics, holding repellent doctrines. Some of these were described in picturesque detail by Peter of Vaux-Sernai, a Cistercian monk of the early thirteenth century:

> First it is to be known that the heretics held that there are two Creators; viz. one of invisible things, whom they called the benevolent God, and another of visible things, whom they named the malevolent God. The New Testament they attributed to the benevolent God; but the Old Testament to the malevolent God, and rejected it altogether, except certain authorities which are inserted in the New Testament from the Old; which, out of reverence to the New Testament, they esteemed worthy of reception. They charged the author of the Old Testament with falsehood, ... They affirmed also, that all the fathers of the Old Testament were damned; that John the Baptist was one of the greater demons. They said also, in their secret doctrine, *(in secreto suo)* that that Christ who was

Gnosticism after Nag Hammadi

born in the visible, and terrestrial Bethlehem, and crucified in Jerusalem, was a bad man, and that Mary Magdalene was his concubine; and that she was the woman taken in adultery, of whom we read in the gospel. For the good Christ, as they said, never ate, nor drank, nor took upon him true flesh, nor ever was in this world, except spiritually in the body of Paul.

.... They preached that Holy Matrimony was meretricious, and that none could be saved in it, if they should beget children. Denying also the Resurrection of the flesh, they invented some unheard of notions, saying, that our souls are those of angelic spirits who, being cast down from heaven by the apostacy of pride, left their glorified bodies in the air; and that these souls themselves, after successively inhabiting seven terrene bodies, of one sort or another, having at length fulfilled their penance, return to those deserted bodies.[32]

What was even more offensive to the Church was their rejection of the sacraments, but this did not concern their converts who were more impressed by the simple lives of the Cathars, which seemed to correspond more nearly with the precepts of the Gospels than did the immorality of many of the Catholic clergy. The Cathar Perfecti – the dedicated Cathars, sure of their salvation, like the Manichaean Elect – strove to live as the Gospel demands. Thus, in 1207, Guilhabert de Castres, the Cathar Bishop of Toulouse, could say:

32 Translated in S.R. Maitland, *Facts and Documents illustrative of the History of the History, Doctrine, and Rites, of the Ancient Albigenses & Waldenses*, London, 1832, pp. 392-394.

Gnosticism and Gnosis: An Introduction

> I have left father, mother and children, I have given up everything the Gospel commands me to renounce, gold and silver I no longer carry in my purse. I am satisfied with each day's food and am not anxious whether tomorrow I shall have the wherewithal to be clothed and fed. You behold in me the beatitudes which Jesus Christ preached and in which His Gospel consists. You see me poor, meek, peaceable, pure in heart, you see me in tears suffering hunger and thirst, persecution and the world's hatred for the sake of Righteousness.[33]

The Cathar Believers, who corresponded to the Manichaean Hearers, lived good but worldly lives in the hope of attaining to the state of the Perfecti by the end of their lives. Prior to their admission into the ranks of Perfecti, they would be expected to confess their sins in the ritual of the Apparelhamentum, of which the following is an extract:

> We have come before God and before you and before the ordinances of the Holy Church that we may receive pardon and penance for all our sins in thought, word and deed from our birth until now and we ask of God mercy and of you that you pray for us to the Holy Father of Mercy that He forgive us.
>
> Let us worship God and declare all our sins and numerous offences in the sight of the Father, the Son and the honoured Holy Spirit, of the honoured Holy Gospels and the honoured Holy

---

[33] Quoted in W.N. Birks and R.A. Gilbert, *The Treasure of Montsegur. A Study of the Cathar Heresy and the Nature of the Cathar Secret.* Loughborough, 1987. p. 56. The authors note that the statement, which was said to have been made during the debate between Cathars and Catholics at Pamiers in 1207, may be apocryphal.

> Apostles, by prayer and faith and by the salvation of all the upright and glorious Christians and blessed ancestors asleep and here present, for their sake we ask you, holy lord, to pardon all our sins. Benedicte, Parcite Nobis. - Amen.[34]

The ritual of admission, the Consolamentum, involved a dialogue – with much reading from the Gospel of John – between the Believer and the Cathar Elder, who advised the Believer of what he or she must accept and what to renounce in the life of a Perfect. At the conclusion of the ceremony the Believer was accepted, in front of witnesses, in the following form:

> And by these witnesses and any others you must keep the commandments of God and hate the world. And if you continue well to the end, we have the hope that your soul shall have life eternal. And the Credent shall say, "I have this will, pray to God for me that He will give me His power"
>
> Witness: "*Parcite Nobis.* Good Christians we pray you by the love of God that you grant this blessing, which God had given you, to our friend here present."
>
> Credent, after making his melioramentum: "*Parcite Nobis.* For all the sins I have ever done in thought, word and deed. I ask pardon of God, of the Church, and of you all."

---

34 From the English translation of the Cathar Rite of the *Apparelhamentum* (General Confession) from the *Lyons Ritual*. Available at (http://www.languedoc-france.info/121204_lyons_apparelhamentum.htm).

Gnosticism and Gnosis: An Introduction

> Assembly of Cathars and Witnesses: "By God and by us and by the Church, may your sins be forgiven and we pray God to forgive you them" *Adoremus, Patrem, et Filium et Spiritum Sanctam.* [Repeated three times][35]

There is, of course, much more to Cathar doctrine, ritual and structure than can be given here, but it is clear that what the Cathars offered was not so much salvation by secret knowledge, as salvation from living the good life. It was certainly a dualist faith, but it differed in many ways from both classical Gnosticism and from Manichaeism. This, however, was not enough to save it from condemnation and destruction.

The initial approach of the Church was by way of preaching and debate, and by the establishment and deployment of religious Orders that emphasised the use of the intellect (the Dominicans) and the living of a truly selfless and spiritual life (the Franciscans). In this way the false beliefs of the Cathars could be combated, and Christian clergy who led blameless lives could become the norm.

But it was not only the Church that opposed the Cathars. The land of the Languedoc was ruled by the Count of Toulouse and his subordinate nobles, and was effectively independent from France – a situation that excited the envy and anger of the French king. When preaching failed, a Crusade was mounted, in 1208, and a long and brutal war ensued, that finally ended after the fall of the Cathar strongholds of Montsegur (1244) and Queribus (1255). In addition, the crusade was followed by a series of Inquisitions that interrogated and punished all

---

[35] From the English Translation of the *Consolamentum* (The Cathar Rite of Baptism by the Holy Spirit) from the *Lyons Ritual*. Available at (http://www.cathar.info/121204_lyons_consolamentum.htm).

suspected Cathars, but showed a fine degree of mercy by burning alive only those Perfecti who refused to recant. The final inquisition, under Jacques Fournier, Bishop of Pamiers and later Pope Benedict XII, came to an end in 1324, and with it the Cathars ceased to be.

Whether or not the Cathars deserve to be classed as gnostic is debatable, but they *were* dualist, and were described by their opponents as Manichaeans. They also fascinate the public today to an even greater degree than do the gnostics. Perhaps they really were the last true gnostics of all.

A coda: gnosis in Britain

Throughout the Middle Ages England, and the rest of the British Isles, seemed to be immune to dualist heresies – just as the early British Church never had to contend with gnostic communities. There have been attempts to identify the decoration of a number of Roman villas in southern Britain as gnostic iconography, but the most that can justly be claimed is that the imagery concerned involves scenes and figures from classical mythology, possibly intermingled with what may be Christian symbols. Scholarly opinion has almost universally rejected any 'gnostic' interpretation.[36]

Evidence for Cathars travelling to England consists principally of Walter Map's derisive remarks, written in the late twelfth century, about the treatment of missionaries of a dualist sect 'called Publicans, or Paterines' (but evidently Cathars). He wrote that,

36   But see, *e.g.*, D. Perring. ' 'Gnosticism' in fourth-century Britain: the Frampton mosaics reconsidered', in *Britannia: a Journal of Romano-British and Kindred Studies*, Vol. XXXIV, 2003, pp. 97-127.

Gnosticism and Gnosis: An Introduction

> To England as yet there have come no more than sixteen, who, by order of King Henry II, were branded and beaten with rods and have disappeared. In Normandy they are not known, nor in Brittany; in Anjou there are many of them, but in Aquitaine and Burgundy they now abound to all infinitude.[37]

There remains one other, curious possibility of a late Cathar presence in England. The writer Nina Epton, who discusses the Cathars in her book *The Valley of Pyrene* (1955), suggested that the communities of the religious Order of Bonshommes in England – at Ashridge in Hertfordshire and Edington in Wiltshire – may have consisted, in part, of Cathar refugees, settled in England in 1285. The origin of the Bonshommes is admittedly obscure, but there is nothing to suggest that their faith was unorthodox and existing archives do not support the idea of secretly surviving Cathars in English religious houses.[38]

What can be said with confidence is that by the end of the fourteenth century, dualism in England and throughout Western Europe had vanished utterly. It would not reappear for another 500 years – and then only as a romantic fiction.

---

37 Walter Map, *De Nugis Curalium*. [Distinction I, Ch. XXX, *c*.1186] Translated by M.R. James. With historical notes by J.E. Lloyd. Edited by E.S. Hartland. London, 1923, p. 63. Map, who became Archdeacon of Oxford in 1197, was a courtier, author and wit during the reign of Henry II.

38 Nina Epton, T*he Valley of Pyrene*. London, 1955, pp. 13-15 & 205-207. For the *Boni Homines*, see Lt. Col. H.F. Chettle, '*The Boni Homines* of Ashridge and Edington', in *The Downside Review*, NS 42-44, 1943–45, pp. 40-55.

Gnosticism after Nag Hammadi

Fig. 6 Henry More

Clinging to the Wreckage:
Gnosticism Today: Revived or Alive?

With the disappearance of the Cathars, 'Christian' gnostic belief systems – indeed, dualist religion in any form – faded away in the West, while in the East only the embattled Mandaeans, still resolutely anti-Christian, kept the dwindling gnostic flame from utter extinction. There remained, however, the myths surrounding the concept of Gnosticism and from the era of the Enlightenment onwards these began to flourish.

Just as the first discoveries of Coptic gnostic texts were taking place, Edward Gibbon was pressing the gnostics into service for his assault upon Christianity in his classic work, *The Decline and Fall of the Roman Empire* (1776). 'The Gnostics', he wrote,

> were distinguished as the most polite, the most learned, and the most wealthy of the Christian name; and that general appellation, which expressed a superiority of knowledge, was either assumed by their own pride, or ironically bestowed by the envy of their adversaries.[1]

He did make other comments less favourable to the gnostics, but this description served to identify them as being intellectually and morally superior to the orthodox. Of course, it wasn't true,

---

1   Edward Gibbon, *The Decline and Fall of the Roman Empire*. Edited by Oliphant Smeaton, London, 1910. Vol. 1, p. 443.

Gnosticism Today

for the gnostics, far from being a social elite, were simply one fragment of the still small Judaeo-Christian community in the Roman Empire. Nor was that community unaware of the need to take account of gnostic speculation. A more accurate overall picture is that given by Kurt Rudolph:

> Moreover, account must be taken of the fact that the Christian Church, by adapting to its environment, and by accepting the legitimate concerns of gnostic theology into its consolidating body of doctrine, developed into a forward-looking ideology and community structure, which ultimately made it heir to the religions of antiquity.[2]

It was Gibbon, however, who had provided an image satisfying to the tastes of avant-garde culture over the next two centuries. The Christian Church and its orthodoxy must represent ignorance, bigotry and social and philosophical oppression; therefore, a system of speculative religious faith that stood up against the Church, and suffered suppression in consequence, must necessarily be spiritually superior to their persecutors, and the gnostics must be revered as spiritual giants; bold pioneers in the quest for absolute spiritual truth. To a dispassionate observer such a view must appear to be absurd, but it has survived and thrived – despite the terrible global wars and the dramatic social changes of the past century.

Why this should be so is unclear; improvements in education have been more than offset by a growing reliance on easily accessible digital mis-information, but this alone cannot explain wilful credulity. Perhaps the urgency of the popular search for

---

2   Rudolph, *op. cit.*, p. 367.

Gnosticism and Gnosis: An Introduction

a 'valid' alternative faith is due in part to the parallel decline of institutional Christianity and the subtle growth of the 'Death of God' scenario of philosophical materialism. Important though the question is, it cannot be addressed here in any depth, but the 'how', 'when' and 'who' of the repackaging of 'Gnosticism' as just such an alternative and superior faith – what might be termed 'gnostic folly' – can be charted, set out and examined.

The rebirth of Gnosticism

The most appropriate starting point for this 'gnostic revival' is 1864, when C.W. King published *The Gnostics and Their Remains, Ancient and Mediaeval*. King was fully conversant with both patristic texts and contemporary studies of Gnosticism, but his expertise was really in the field of ancient gemstones, especially 'gnostic' and magical amulets, and his speculations about the gnostics are pure flights of fancy. He relates them to the Knights Templar and the freemasons and maintains that Gnosticism 'may be traced up to Indian speculative philosophy, as its genuine fountain-head' (p. vi), while 'the later Gnosticism' is 'the spirit of Asiatic antiquity endeavouring to usurp the empire over the human soul by insinuating itself into the Christian Church' (p. 4). The Church, however, failed to comprehend it:

> The Christian writers, who have treated upon the origin and nature of these doctrines, were (Origen excepted) ignorant ecclesiastics, who could discern nothing in any religion beyond its outside forms, which they construed in the worst possible sense.[3]

---

3   *op. cit.*, p. 5.

Gnosticism Today

Ten years later this approach found favour with H.P. Blavatsky, the co-founder of the Theosophical Society, when she compiled her first major work, *Isis Unveiled* (1877), in which she quotes King's opinions with approval. For the gnostics themselves she has little but admiration; they were, 'the only heirs to whose share had fallen a few stray crumbs of the unadulterated truth of primitive Christianity', even though, she notes elsewhere, 'the primitive pure Oriental gnosticism was completely corrupted and degraded by the different subsequent sects'.[4] Later she would argue that the true, inner gnosis could 'only be obtained by Initiation into the Spiritual Mysteries'.[5] This she did not pretend to offer, any more than did her disciple G.R.S. Mead, who was a real scholar and the author of a series of studies of gnostic beliefs. But Mead could not escape the less than objective attitudes of his theosophical milieu and said of the gnostics that,

> The Gnostic mind rapidly arrived on the one hand at many conclusions which the Catholics gradually adopted only after generations of hesitation, and on the other at a number of conclusions which even to our present generation seem too premature.[6]

He also seemed occasionally to be prefiguring the ersatz spirituality of the New Age, as when he writes that,

> [The Gnostics] strove for the knowledge of God, the science of realities, the gnosis of things-that-

---

4 H.P. Blavatsky, *Isis Unveiled*. New York [& London], 1877, Vol. 2, p. 249; Vol. 1, p. 271.

5 Blavatsky, *The Theosophical Glossary*. London, 1892, p. 129.

6 G.R.S. Mead, *Fragments of a Faith Forgotten, Sketches among the Gnostics, Mainly of the First Two Centuries*. London, 1900, p. 136.

are; wisdom was their goal; the holy things of life their study. ... Gnosis is not the end – it is the beginning of the path, the end is God – and hence the Gnostics would be those who used the Gnosis as the means to set their feet upon the Way to God.[7]

Such an approach has been followed by more recent theosophists. For example, Duncan Greenlees, writing in 1958, could claim that far from being Christian,

> Gnosticism is a system of direct experiential knowledge of God and the nature of the Soul and the universe; therefore it has no fixed dogmas or creed but naturally expresses itself in terms familiar to its environment.

That,

> [Gnostics] were long falsely styled Christian heretics ... So long as we knew nothing of them beyond what the not-so-clever refutators of the age of controversy (late 2nd to 5th centuries A.D.) chose to transmit, badly garbled, there was some excuse for this misunderstanding.

And that,

> In the 'Gnosis' that we know, the Christian elements are mostly over-writing or editing of earlier 'pagan' forms which had lost their appeal in the 'sceptical' age of the decline of myth.[8]

---

7   *ibid.* p. 32.

8   Duncan Greenlees (Ed. & trans.), *The World Gospel Series. 13. The Gospel of the Gnostics.* Adyar, 1958. pp. vii, xi & xii.

Gnosticism Today

It is, however, all very theoretical, but there were others, within and around the theosophical movement, who wished to put their understanding of the gnosis into a practical form and in a more or less Christian context. They were inspired by Anna Kingsford, a contemporary of Mme Blavatsky, who disliked the eastern bias of the Theosophical Society and developed a specifically Christian form of Theosophy based on revelations that she collated and published in her book *The Perfect Way* (1882). She looked upon her newly recovered religious system of the ancients as 'the basic and secret doctrine of all the great religions of antiquity, including Christianity, – the doctrine commonly called the Gnosis, and variously entitled Hermetic and Kabbalistic'.[9]

Among those inspired by Anna Kingsford was Marie, Countess of Caithness, who was also estranged from Theosophy and sought revelations of her own within her private spiritualist circle. Late in 1889 the circle was visited by the spirit of Guilhabert de Castres, the greatest of the Cathar bishops, who urged the sitters to establish a revived 'Gnostic Church'. One of them, Jules Doinel, an archivist who was already involved with many esoteric bodies, did precisely that.

The Gnostic Church

Within a year Doinel had established the Nouvelle Église Gnostique, with himself as Patriarch under the name of Tau Valentin II (after the gnostic teacher, Valentinus). His church did not resemble any gnostic church of the past; it was quasi-

---

[9] Kingsford [and Edward Maitland], *The Perfect Way; or, the Finding of Christ*. London, 1882, p. i.

masonic in its ethos and its liturgy was derived from that of the Cathars. It was also closely linked to the Martinist Order, the head of which, Papus (Gérard Encausse), Doinel had promptly consecrated as a bishop. Other prominent French occultists – including ladies, for the church followed Cathar practice in having both male and female clergy – rapidly followed and in its own small way the Gnostic Church prospered.

As a church designed for the elite few it suffered great embarrassment in 1895 when Doinel left his creation, entered the Church of Rome and wrote a damning exposé, *Lucifer Démasqué* (Lucifer Unmasked).[10] Despite its hostility, Doinel's book is a valuable source of information about his church – to which he returned in 1900 and in which he remained quietly until his death in 1902. The exposé did the church no harm and it continued to grow until, as is the way with such bodies, it began to split.

Doinel was followed as patriarch by Léonce Fabre des Essarts (Tau Synesius), under whom the first division occurred. In 1906 Joanny Bricaud (Tau Jean II) left the church and established the Église Catholique Gnostique at Lyon a year later, changing its name rapidly to Église Gnostique Universelle. Synesius, however, retained the support of Papus (Gérard Encausse), who introduced the young René Guénon and set him up in 1909 as editor of *La Gnose*, which was effectively a house journal of the Gnostic Church, although within a few years Guénon had turned from Gnosticism to Sufism.

10   There is no English translation of *Lucifer Démasqué*, but A.E. Waite gives an amusing and perceptive summary in his *Devil Worship in France*. (London, 1896). The best study of the Gnostic Church is René Le Forestier, *L'Occultisme en France aux XIXème et XXème siècles. L'Église Gnostique*. Milan, 1990. Edited by Antoine Faivre.

Gnosticism Today

The church also underwent a variety of transformations. Through its Martinist and masonic connections the Lyon church had brought in a variety of odd and eccentric occultists – Theodor Reuss, Aleister Crowley and H. Spencer Lewis among them – and departed decisively from the original Cathar model. However, the extant Église Gnostique Universelle retains a gnostic ethos and abjures utterly the self-obsessed and sexual emphases of the Ecclesia Gnostica Catholica with its repellent mass written by Crowley.

These varied bodies do not exhaust the range of 'Gnostic Churches'; there is also the Ecclesia Gnostica – originally named the Pre-Nicene Gnostic Catholic Church – that was founded in England in 1953 by Richard, Duc de Palatine (Ronald Powell), who sought to 'restore the Gnosis - Divine Wisdom to the Christian Church'. De Palatine remained as Presiding Bishop of this church until his death in 1977, when he was succeeded in office by Stephan A. Hoeller, who had built up the church in Los Angeles since 1959. Hoeller has also linked his church to The Gnostic Society, an organisation founded in 1928 by two American theosophists, and through the society's 'Gnosis Archive' has given the church a prominent and respected Internet presence.

It is perhaps unnecessary to state that none of these gnostic churches resemble the various schools of the early centuries. Hoeller sees Gnosticism as a very early form of Christianity, but unlike the orthodox church,

> It is much more individualistic. It is more oriented toward the personal, spiritual advancement and transformation of the individual, and regards

figures such as Jesus as being helpers rather than sacrificial saviors.[11]

We should thus not be surprised that for Hoeller,

> Here, in the Gnostic Mass, the intention is primarily to elevate and to transform the worshipper's consciousness so as to attain a liberating insight – gnosis. It is not primarily connected with re-enacting the sacrificial death of Jesus Christ on the cross.[12]

Just as distinct from Christian orthodoxy is the viewpoint of the Lectorium Rosicrucianum, an organisation devoted to both Gnosticism and Christian Esotericism, which was founded in the Netherlands in 1945 by two modern Rosicrucians, Jan van Rijckenborgh (Jan Leene) and Catharose de Petri (Henny Stok-Huyser). In their eyes Rosicrucianism is Gnosticism reborn, and illuminated by the neo-Catharism that they discovered to be thriving in southern France. To further these ends they established the 'Young Gnostic Brotherhood' in 1957 and opened a 'Galaad Centre' at Ussat-les-Bains in the Languedoc.[13] But those who join the Lectorium do not come to it by accident. According to Catharose de Petri, 'We have been led to the Gnosis by the karmic urge of our aural being', this – even for this select band of initiates – being the result of our guilt over failings in past lives. But the gnostic has been marked as such

---

[11] 'The Suppressed Teachings of Gnosticism. Robert Guffey interviews Dr. Stephan Hoeller', in *Paranoia Magazine*, No. 34, Winter 2004, p.29.

[12] *ibid.* p. 35.

[13] The Young Gnostic Brotherhood is no longer based at Ussat, the Galaad Centre having closed in 1968.

Gnosticism Today

and is predestined for the gnosis, and when he responds to its call he will answer: 'By myself I am nothing, O Gnosis; have mercy upon me, a sinner!'[14] In effect this is reincarnation and salvation in one fell swoop.

Gnosticism in modern culture

There is also a degree of popular and intellectual enthusiasm for gnostic ideas outside the confines of religious practice and academic study. Gnostic references and themes have been utilised occasionally by a number of writers from the late nineteenth century onwards – and have been found in the work of many others by enthusiasts who have such a gift of discernment that they can identify gnostic elements even where the authors concerned have had no conscious awareness or intention of employing them.

Thus it is that poets as varied as William Blake, W.B. Yeats and Robert Frost have all been labelled, on occasion, as gnostics – but the judgement is necessarily subjective and also highly equivocal. Even in the case of Herman Melville, whose short poem, 'Fragments of a Lost Gnostic Poem of the Twelfth Century', does have gnostic, or rather Cathar, references, it should be recognised that he wrote for poetic effect, not to express his personal belief. However, in Melville's masterpiece, *Moby Dick*, Ahab's hatred of the whale is presented by Ishmael as a rage against the Demiurge of the ancient Ophites. But all

---

14 See the untitled collection of essays, *Catharose de Petri*. Haarlem, 1981, pp. 52 & 58.

that this shows is that Melville knew about the gnostics, not that he shared their faith.[15]

This is also true of Lawrence Durrell, whose four novels of 'The Alexandria Quartet' (*Justine, Balthazar, Mountolive* and *Clea*) do contain gnostic references that are relevant to their plots. Durrell was certainly fascinated by the gnostics – he wrote a laudatory preface to Jacques Lacarrière's brief, elegiac study, *Les Gnostiques* (1973) – but he had gained his knowledge of them from E.M. Forster's *Alexandria: A History and a Guide* (1922) and he did not subscribe to gnostic beliefs. The gnostics were simply pressed into service, together with other esoteric beliefs, in novels that concern the complexities and tribulations of the human condition.

Durrell's friend, Henry Miller, also contributed to Lacarrière's book and he has often been labelled as a 'gnostic', although this is a loose use of the term and is applied not because Miller was a gnostic, but as a reflection of his libertarianism and rejection of orthodox mores. Of course, there are writers who have gone beyond simple reference and have deliberately utilised gnostic beliefs and doctrines in their work. The most

---

15 The poem, 'Fragments', which is an invention, appears in Melville's *Timoleon* (1891):
   Found a family, build a state,
   The pledged event is still the same:
   Matter in end will never abate
   His ancient brutal claim.

   Indolence is heaven's ally here,
   And energy the child of hell:
   The Good Man pouring from his pitcher clear
   But brims the poisoned well.

striking exemplar is the literary critic Harold Bloom, who was not only predisposed to see Gnosticism in the work of almost every writer he studied, but also wrote an odd science fiction novel, *The Flight to Lucifer: a Gnostic Fantasy* (1979), which is suffused with gnostic concepts and characters.[16]

More successful as science fiction is Philip K. Dick's novel *VALIS* (1981), which contains a significant and overt gnostic content. However, this content is not central to his more famous novel *Do Androids Dream of Electric Sheep?* (1968), on which the film *Blade Runner* (1982) is based. Neither book nor film is 'gnostic', despite claims that they are, and should be seen rather as reflecting the author's concerns with dystopias, malignant autocrats and the human creation of artificial human beings.

Gnostic ideas have been perceived as a significant influence on a number of popular films. Perhaps, as argued by the critic Eric Wilson, because film is the ideal medium for presenting gnostic ideas.

> What does an utterly illusory form have to do with a worldview committed to the idea that all matter is unreal and that truth – gnosis, intimate acquaintance – exists far beyond the turning planets? .... Is it possible that its tenuous reality makes film an especially apt vehicle for purveying Gnostic notions of a false universe – the world as the dream of an evil god? Is it conceivable that cinema, because of its self-consuming contradictions ... is

16 Bloom modelled his story on David Lindsay's novel, *A Voyage to Arcturus* (1920), which also involves a world created by a Demiurge, although there are no overt gnostic references in the text.

Gnosticism and Gnosis: An Introduction

an eminently powerful medium for transcending the conflicts of time to life beyond clocks?[17]

But gnostic themes and concepts tend to be employed because directors find them to be useful adjuncts to pessimistic portrayals of a dystopian future or as a reflection of their own despairing or nihilistic views of society. For example, *The Truman Show* (1998) has been claimed as a parallel of the creation of this world by a Demiurge. But the setting of the film is merely a microcosm – only the hero of the eponymous television show is ignorant of the unreality of his world. The maker of the show cannot truly be seen as a Demiurge, for he is broadcasting it as entertainment to a vast audience that is fully aware that it is fantasy. Nor can *The Matrix* (1999) and its successors be accepted as being 'gnostic' in any meaningful sense. Although they utilise gnostic ideas, the aim of these films is essentially to portray the corruption and evil of totalitarian society and the shifting boundaries between simulated and objective reality.

In general terms, Gnosticism has been less of an influence upon writers, artists and critics than a source of ideas and terminology to be drawn upon – plundered, if you will – as part of their creative processes. Thus, the Buddhist scholar Edward Conze entitled his autobiography *The Memoirs of a Modern Gnostic* (1979), not because he perceived himself as a gnostic, but because it seemed fitting for one who believed that he had been truly enlightened, via Buddhism, and was a part of an intellectual elite.

17 Eric G. Wilson, *Secret Cinema: Gnostic Vision in Film*. New York, 2006, pp. 2-3.

Gnosticism Today

There have also been scholars for whom Gnosticism was an identifiable influence upon their work, if not upon their lives. Perhaps the most famous of these is the psychologist C.G. Jung, who perceived the gnostics as primitive explorers of the unconscious mind. Jung wrote that,

> Between 1918 and 1926 I had seriously studied the Gnostic writers, for they too had been confronted with the primal world of the unconscious and had dealt with its contents, with images that were obviously contaminated with the world of instinct. .... But the Gnostics were too remote for me to establish any link with them in regard to the questions that were confronting me.[18]

However, when he began to study alchemy, Jung realised that: 'I had stumbled upon the historical counterpart of my psychology of the unconscious. The possibility of a comparison with alchemy, and the uninterrupted intellectual chain back to Gnosticism gave substance to my psychology.'[19]

At this time, 1925, Jung wrote his *Seven Sermons to the Dead*, a short work for private circulation, in which he adopts the persona of the gnostic teacher Basilides and shows his familiarity with the concepts and technical vocabulary of the gnostics. The text, however, is concerned with the unconscious mind. Jung does not preach gnostic tenets, but emphasises the need for individuation: self-realisation here and now rather than escape from matter.

18 C.G. Jung, *Memories, Dreams, Reflections*. London, 1963, p. 192.
19 *idem*. p. 196.

Gnosticism and Gnosis: An Introduction

Another of Jung's 'private' works was his unfinished '*Red Book*', 'a folio volume bound in red leather', in which he set down 'an aesthetic elaboration of my fantasies', as a fine calligraphic text illustrated by many coloured 'mandala drawings'.[20] Although this was purely subjective material, it helped him to develop his theories of archetypes, individuation and the collective unconscious; but although it requires a great stretching of meaning to label it a 'gnostic' work, the *Red Book* has been seized upon by modern gnostics as a quarry to be worked for their promotion of Gnosticism – as they perceive it to be.

Gnosis and gnostics at the present day

A desire to know the source of our being, the origin of the universe and our place and purpose within it seems to be an inherent part of the human condition. But why turn to gnostic beliefs and ideas for answers? What is the appeal of Gnosticism – which is a system of religious speculation, rather than a way of life in this world – that it should today be so eagerly embraced by so many as a spiritual path, and so intently studied by scholars? There is no obvious, single answer, but whereas the fascination for the scholar may be due to a simple desire for the pursuit of knowledge, the enthusiasm of the general public has a different source. The popular quest is for a spiritual path and that now tends to be increasingly sought outside the confines of organised religion. This, in turn, is related to a general decline in communal activities and community engagement, which has been exacerbated by the rise of digital communication and the increasing isolation of the individual that comes in its wake.

---

20   *idem.* p. 180.

Gnosticism Today

In the absence of institutional spiritual practice, the spiritual seeker turns most readily to a path that can be attuned to the solitary individual. Gnosticism, in the popular imagination, is thus an ideal solution to the spiritual quest. Such a simplistic explanation cannot alone explain the appeal of Gnosticism, but it is a significant factor and will suffice for the present.

Although it is an institution, the Gnostic Church of today answers to the individualist need. It is not, and does not claim to be, a survival of ancient Gnosticism. It was the product of the chaotic, and generally ill-informed, nineteenth-century counter-culture, and reflects a misunderstanding, by its founders and followers, of what was then known or speculated about the gnostics by scholars of the time. More recently they have tended to confuse mysticism, or rather mystical experience, with the presumed spiritual experiences of historical gnostics. But their view of gnosis is from a modern, not an ancient perspective:

> Gnosis [is] the knowledge of transcendence arrived at by way of interior, intuitive means. ... Gnosticism expresses a specific religious experience, an experience that does not lend itself to the language of theology or philosophy, but which is instead closely affinitized [sic] to, and expresses itself through, the medium of myth.[21]

Today we possess far more original gnostic texts, and other, related ancient texts, and can engage in more informed speculation than was possible in 1890 about the structure, identity and distribution of the various gnostic schools and

---

21 Stephan A. Hoeller, '*The Gnostic World View: A Brief Summary of Gnosticism*'. The Gnosis Archive, (1995) (http://www.gnosis.org/gnintro.htm).

Gnosticism and Gnosis: An Introduction

belief systems. But our knowledge and understanding of gnostic beliefs and of the social, economic and cultural conditions in which those belief systems originated and developed is by no means comprehensive and is far from being complete.

However, what we have learned has enabled church historians and biblical scholars to speculate on the complex relationship between the 'orthodox' early Church and what may be termed gnostic forms of Christianity. Some of these arguments, and the conclusions drawn from them, call – in the eyes of their proponents, at least – for radical rethinking of the progress of the early Church and of the very nature of what they prefer to term 'Christianities'.

Their enthusiasm can lead them to present as certainties what are in fact, tentative speculations, and to exhibit a degree of hostility to orthodox understanding of the Christian faith. Thus Professor Bart D. Ehrman has argued, in presenting a series of lectures for 'The Great Courses', that only one group 'amongst many competing Christianities won the struggle for dominance', enabling it to determine which beliefs are 'central to the faith'; to 'rewrite the history of Christianity's internal conflicts'; and to 'produce a canon of sacred texts – the New Testament – that supported its own views'.[22] This viewpoint is itself highly contentious, but authors may be excused for believing their own arguments. Also contentious are the arguments of Elaine Pagels and others, based largely on Nag Hammadi texts, for a prominent role played by women in the earliest Christian decades.

---

22   The lectures, *'From Jesus to Constantine: A History of Early Christianity'* (2011) are published by the Great Courses company as compact audio discs. The phrases quoted are from promotional text for the series.

Gnosticism Today

Such views tend to be accompanied by an acceptance of a very early date for at least some of the Nag Hammadi gospels and other texts. It should be stressed, however, that there is no certain dating of any gnostic or apocryphal New Testament text before the late second century AD – almost a century later than the canonical Gospels, Acts and Epistles. We must, of course, accept and encourage scholarly debate, which can only enrich our understanding of early Christianity and its milieu, but in that debate we must not lose sight of objectivity. The following episode makes clear the perils of doing so.

We do know that some apocryphal Gospels and Acts are late and blatant forgeries, although dating from the early centuries. One such gospel fragment, that challenged traditional views on the Gospel of Mark, the earliest of the Synoptic Gospels, has proved to be a modern forgery – and almost certainly the work of its discoverer, the eminent biblical scholar, Morton Smith. The story of this '*Secret Gospel of Mark*' was presented to the academic world in a monograph published in 1973,[23] and despite its controversial nature, it was accepted by many as casting a damaging light on traditional orthodoxy. More than thirty years later, in 2007, Smith's deception and forgery were finally exposed in a magisterial work by Peter Jeffery.[24] There are, however, still scholars who are reluctant to jettison the forged text.

23 Morton Smith, *Clement of Alexandria and a Secret Gospel of Mark*. Cambridge, Harvard UP, 1973.

24 Peter Jeffery, *The Secret Gospel of Mark Unveiled: Imagined Rituals of Sex, Death, and Madness in a Biblical Forgery*. New Haven, Yale UP, 2007.

Gnosticism and Gnosis: An Introduction

This episode is, admittedly, not directly related to gnostic texts – all of which are genuinely ancient – but it emphasises the need to exercise caution before attempting to alter ancient reality with the benefit of what may prove to be imperfect hindsight. Debate in the fields of gnostic, biblical and early Christian studies is all too often lamentably acrimonious, but it must be stressed that, apart from Morton Smith, no scholar working in these fields has ever displayed anything but impeccable integrity.

As a legitimate area of scholarly research, Gnosticism is a fascinating subject that can appeal to the intelligent layman as much as to the professional academic. Nor is that the limit of its appeal. Adherents of 'New Age' spirituality are also drawn to gnostic texts that seem, to them, to offer a form of Christianity that demands no adherence to dogma and permits the believer to decide for him or herself just which doctrines to accept or reject. Of such texts, the most popular for the New Age community seems to be *The Gospel of Thomas*, perhaps because it is a simple collection of sayings, shorn of any narrative content and divorced from a wider biblical context – and from which agreeable sayings of Jesus can be selected at will. It is undeniable that study of the sayings in *The Gospel of Thomas*, and in other Nag Hammadi texts, has cast new light and stimulated debate on our interpretation and understanding of the life and work of the historical Jesus, but the canonical Scriptures form a coherent whole, and it is sad that so many 'alternative spiritual seekers' (for want of a better expression), are ignorant of both the Old and the New Testaments, which they seem to feel are somehow inferior to the gnostic scriptures.

Gnosticism Today

But is Gnosticism in its modern dress compatible with orthodox Christianity? It has become a commonplace for 'alternative' writers on Gnosticism to justify the selective reading of gnostic scriptures by promoting them as representing 'the path of the Gnostics in the early centuries of Christianity, before the orthodox Church labelled their teachings heresy and forced their practices underground.'[25] Such statements do not give an imprimatur to gnostic texts; they simply betray the ignorance of these writers. Christianity in its traditional, catholic form was not imposed upon unwilling communities, and a real knowledge of church history would demonstrate that gnostic 'practices' were not 'forced underground'. It was rather the case that the gnostics remained in active competition with orthodoxy until the eventual suppression of non-Christian religions by the Roman authorities at the close of the fourth century. Roman persecution before this time had been directed principally against orthodox Christianity. Nor should it be forgotten that decisions by church authorities as to what comprises the Canon of Scripture were arrived at only after long debate; these were not the decisions of a minority and they were imposed neither arbitrarily nor abruptly.

Of course, if a non-Christian chooses to take up Gnosticism, then he or she cannot be expected to have much concern for the niceties of church history, or of the Christian faith. What, then, is the appeal of Gnosticism for such a person? Modern 'Gnosticism' does not offer a systematic theology, nor a clearly defined philosophy. It is not offered as path to salvation, but as a way of attaining heightened religious experience, solely for the

---

25 From the promotional synopsis of Alan Jacobs, *Essential Gnostic Gospels*. London, 2006.

Gnosticism and Gnosis: An Introduction

benefit of the self. There is an implicit rejection of the notion of sin, because the world's failings lie with the Creator not within creation, which suggests that moral codes are arbitrary and a matter for individual choice. It is, however, unlikely that the would-be gnostic will reflect that such a state of being would demolish the entire foundation of society, which cannot function without an agreed set of rules.

Given the above, modern gnostics are seen to be following a self-indulgent spiritual path that avoids the discipline and humanity of the great religions. Such a path cannot fit with any orthodox form of Christianity: it is devoid of compassion (contrary to the teachings of Christ or Buddha); it is self-centred and denies that there is anything of value in the material world. Some, not least the popular 'gnostic' authors and teachers, will deny that this is their stance, but the logic of their stated beliefs points inexorably in this direction.

The approach of contemporary gnostics differs, of course, from that of their claimed forebears. For the most part, gnostics of the early centuries had a real desire for spiritual attainment, for a direct experience of God that they believed would come to them by virtue of the saving knowledge that was granted to them because of their privileged, spiritual natures. Such a desire can be understood, but it is elitist and exclusive – only those possessed of gnosis can be saved – and it is this that, in the last analysis, distinguished them from everyday, orthodox Christians. As it still does.

Modern gnostics may argue that theirs is the 'true' Christianity, and that the Christian faith as it should

Gnosticism after Nag Hammadi

have been – as Christ wished it to be – was usurped by the machinations of the Church Fathers. But this flies in the face of both history and reason. What matters is not what might have been, but what actually did happen. Orthodoxy triumphed over what it perceived as heresy, not because it was imposed by an unrepresentative clique, but because it was a system of beliefs and practices that was freely given and freely received. It succeeded because it was the faith that ordinary Christians wished for and accepted. Social and political attitudes change, and in this respect the Church, or rather Churches, have altered over the centuries, but the orthodox model of Christianity – a fully working model with the central tenets unchanged – is what we still have today. It is also integrated with the world in a way that Gnosticism never could be. Christianity recognises the need to address both the spiritual and the material aspects of human culture, and so, whereas the Gnostic cosmology was pre-scientific and has long been exploded, the orthodox view of the material universe is rather, a-scientific and is adaptable to the current, prevailing view of the nature of that universe. Christianity is not a scientific discipline, but a faith, and although it cannot deny historical fact it applies non-empirical methods as far as philosophical and spiritual analysis and debate are concerned.

This is not to say that we who are Christians should be as dismissive as Plotinus or as vitriolic as the Church Fathers in our assessment of Gnosticism, but we must recognise that it remains a form of faith that is incompatible with orthodox Christianity. Gnosticism failed as a world religion because

Gnosticism and Gnosis: An Introduction

it was world-denying (in a broader sense than self-denial), whereas Christianity has always been world affirming. It also has its own form of gnosis: a profound insight into our personal relationship with God that comes with faith through the action of divine Grace. And this gnosis is distinguished from that of the gnostic – whose exclusive, saving knowledge is confined to himself alone – by expressing itself in following Christ's Great Commandment, to love God and to love your neighbour as yourself. For those who hold to the Christian faith it is a distinction between gnosis and agape, which was summed up neatly and completely by Paul (1 Cor. 8:1):

'Knowledge puffs up, but Love builds up.'

Further Reading

The bibliography of Gnosticism is vast and many of the texts, commentaries and studies are highly technical. Many of them are also expensive – especially the volumes of the Nag Hammadi Studies series – and difficult to obtain, but the books on the following annotated list, which is designed for English-speaking readers who wish for greater depth and detail for the topics covered above, are for the most part both readily accessible and fully comprehensible. Bibliographical details of other, more specialised works, referred to in the text, are given in the relevant footnotes.

(a) Texts

Foerster, W. *Gnosis: A selection of Gnostic Texts*.
> English translation edited by R. McL. Wilson. Oxford, 1972-74, 2 vols. A valuable collection of both patristic texts on Gnosticism and original Coptic and Mandaic sources, all with concise introductions.

Hultgren, Arland J. & Haggmark, S.A. (Ed)
> *The Earliest Christian Heretics. Readings from their Opponents*. Minneapolis, 1996.

Kee, Howard Clark *The Origins of Christianity. Sources and Documents*. London, 1980. A collection that sets Christianity in its contemporary context.

Gnosticism and Gnosis: An Introduction

Layton, Bentley *The Gnostic Scriptures: A New Translation with Annotations and Introductions.* London, 1987. A substantial collection of texts from the Nag Hammadi codices and patristic sources. Layton's translations are in many ways more appealing than those in the various complete editions of the Nag Hammadi texts.

Mead, G.R.S. (Trans.) *Pistis Sophia, a Gnostic Miscellany: being for the Most Part extracts from the Books of the Saviour.* Revised edition, 1921. An edition that has been superseded, but it remains serviceable and it is readily available online (http://www.sacred-texts.com), whereas the modern scholarly edition of Violet Macdermot (1978) is difficult to find and very expensive.

Meyer, Marvin (Ed.) *The Nag Hammadi Scriptures.* New York, 2007. The most recent, and fully annotated, edition of the Nag Hammadi texts in English translation, but it does not include *Pistis Sophia* or the Bruce codex.

Schneemelcher, Wilhelm *New Testament Apocrypha.* Revised edition. English translation edited by R. McL. Wilson. Cambridge, 1991, 1992, 2 vols. Volume 1: Gospels and related Writings; Volume 2: Writings relating to the Apostles, Apocalypses and related subjects.

(b) Studies

Gilbert, R.A. (Ed.) *Knowledge of the Heart: Gnostic Movements & Secret Traditions.* Transactions of the Eighth International Conference ... 2006. The Canonbury Papers Volume 5. London, 2008. A collection of twelve papers that consider Gnosticism in the context of both the ancient world and in more recent currents of thought.

Further Reading

King, Karen L. *What is Gnosticism?*
Cambridge, MA, 2003. A detailed general survey that considers in depth the changing scholarly attitudes and approaches to Gnosticism over the last hundred years.

Koester, Helmut *Ancient Christian Gospels Their History and Development.* London, 1990. A comprehensive study that sets the gnostic gospels in their contemporary context.

Logan, Alastair H.B. *Gnostic Truth and Christian Heresy: A Study in the History of Gnosticism.* Edinburgh, 1996. A challenging view of Gnosticism that concentrates on the Jewish origin of these belief systems and on the significance of their impact on Christianity.

Meyer, Marvin *The Gnostic Discoveries: The Impact of the Nag Hammadi Library.* San Francisco, 2005.

Pagels, Elaine *The Gnostic Gospels.* New York, 1979.
A very readable introduction and general survey by an eminent scholar of Gnosticism. It is, however, coloured to some extent by the author's personal beliefs and attitudes.

Pearson, Birger *Ancient Gnosticism: Traditions and Literature.*
Minneapolis, 2007. An excellent general study designed for both students and the lay public.

Perkins, Pheme *Gnosticism and the New Testament.*
Minneapolis, 1993. A sound and thorough account of the changing relationships between Christianity and Gnosticism in the early centuries of the Christian era.

Pétrement, Simone *A Separate God: The Christian Origins of Gnosticism.* London, 1991. An uncompromising, scholarly presentation of what has become an unfashionable thesis.

Gnosticism and Gnosis: An Introduction

Rudolph, Kurt *Gnosis, the Nature and History of an Ancient Religion*. Edinburgh, 1983. A very detailed survey that that provides an excellent scholarly overview. The author tends to look upon Gnosticism as a discrete religion – a view that is now generally rejected.

Turner, John D. & Anne McGuire (Ed) *The Nag Hammadi Library after Fifty Years*. Proceedings of the 1995 Society of Biblical Literature Commemoration. Leiden, 1997. Twenty-two papers covering the development of Nag Hammadi research and detailed studies of specific texts. It has a full and excellent bibliography.

Williams, Michael *Rethinking "Gnosticism" An Argument for Dismantling a Dubious Category*. Princeton UP, 1996. A truly ground-breaking study that sparked controversy and stimulated much further research.

Yamauchi, Edwin *Pre-Christian Gnosticism: A Survey of the Proposed Evidences*. 1973. He concludes that there are no gnostic texts before the late first century AD.

(c) Modern 'Gnosticism'

There is a very substantial literature of the various contemporary schools of thought that seek to promote modern forms of 'Gnosticism', which often bear no resemblance to its classical form. Much of this literature is ill-informed, superficial and tendentious, but there are also serious and intelligent proponents of Gnosticism in its modern dress, of whom Stephan Hoeller is probably the best known. He is the director of the 'Gnostic Society' and Regionary Bishop, for America, of the Ecclesia Gnostica. The best source for information on modern

Further Reading

Gnosticism is the online 'Gnosis Archive' (www.gnosis.org). The following titles will provide an introduction for those who wish to read further on this topic.

Hoeller, Stephan A. *Gnosticism: New Light on the Ancient Tradition of Inner Knowing.* Wheaton, 2002. Hoeller is the most prominent contemporary advocate for neo-Gnosticism,

Jung, Carl Gustav, *VII Sermones ad Mortuos. The Seven Sermons to the Dead written by Basilides in Alexandria the City where the East toucheth the West.* Privately printed, 1925 [Reprinted London, 1967].

Le Forestier, René *L'Occultisme en France aux XIXème et XXème siècles. L'Église Gnostique.* Milan 1990. Edited by Antoine Faivre. There is no adequate study of the Gnostic Church in English.

Smith, Richard, 'The Modern Relevance of Gnosticism', in: J.M. Robinson, *The Nag Hammadi Library in English.* San Francisco, 1988, 3rd ed pp. 532-549.

Wilson, Eric G. *Secret Cinema: Gnostic Vision in Film.* New York, 2006, An intelligent and perceptive study of Gnosticism in the most pervasive aspect of popular culture.

Gnosticism and Gnosis: An Introduction

Index

A

Abrasax 57
Achamoth 44, 53
Act of Peter 30
Acts of the Apostles 19, 23
Adam 45, 46, 63, 65, 79, 81, 85, 94
Adversus Haereses, 40, 43, 58
aeons 40, 42, 51, 52, 63
Akhmim 30
Albi 96
Albigenses 96, 97
Alcibiades 74
Alexandria 7, 17, 27, 35, 45, 46, 48, 57, 58, 62, 63, 64, 67, 69, 72, 114, 121, 131
Alexandria Quartet 114
Algeria 84
Alice 8
alpha 48
androgynous 42
angels 41, 43, 45, 55, 56, 59, 63
Anglican 21
antinomian 54, 56, 58, 59
Antioch 56, 57
Aphrodite 45
Apocalypse of Adam 65
Apocrypha 21, 70, 128
Apocryphon of John 30, 41, 65
apostles 7, 19, 23, 99, 128
Apparelhamentum 98, 99
Aquitaine 102
archegos 87
archons 41, 51, 53, 58

Armenia 91, 92
Ashridge 102
Asia Minor 17, 33, 36, 72, 92
Askew, Anthony 29, 132
Assiut 84
astrology 74, 75
Athanasius 69, 70
Attridge 29
Augustine 26, 28, 29, 83
Autogenes 41
Axionicus 62

B

Babylonian exile 17
Bahram I 82
Balkans 94
baptism 47, 62, 100
Barbelo 41, 42
Bardaisan 75, 76, 77
Bardesanes 62
Basilides 27, 56, 57, 58, 59, 91, 117, 131
Basilidians 27
Baur, Walter 33, 34
beatitudes 98
Bema, The 88
Berlin Museum 30
Bible 12, 14, 18, 19
Birger Pearson 13
Bishop 27, 28, 69, 95, 96, 98, 101, 111, 130
Bishop of Pamiers 101
Blake 113, 139
Blake, William 113
Blavatsky H.P. 107, 109
Bloom 115, 135

Index

Bloom, Harold 115
Bodleian Library 30
Bogomil 92, 93, 94, 96
Bogomils 90, 91, 92, 94, 95
Book of the Laws of Countries 75
Books of Jeu 30
Bousset W. 16
Bricaud, Joanny 110, 135
bridal chamber 46, 47, 50
British Museum 30
Brittany 102
Bruce Codex 6, 4, 51
Bruce, James 6, 4, 30, 51, 128, 135
Buddhism 87, 116
Burgundy 102
Bythos 40, 44, 64
Byzantine Empire 87, 90, 94

C

Cainites 27
Cairo 31
Canaanite 48
Cancik, Hubert 72, 135
Canon 18, 19, 32, 123
Capernaum 61
Carcassonne 96
Carpocrates 58, 59
Cathar Church 96
Catharose de Petri 112, 113
Cathar Perfecti 98
Cathar refugees 102
Cathars 95, 96, 97, 98, 100, 101, 102, 104, 110
Celsus 28, 52
Central Asia 82, 84, 87, 90
ceremonial 50, 53

Chaldean 75
chrism 47, 64
Christ 23, 30, 37, 46, 47, 49, 56, 57, 58, 60, 61, 63, 65, 74, 75, 76, 79, 81, 91, 97, 98, 109, 112, 124, 126
Christian Church 5, 25, 38, 86, 90, 105, 106, 111
Christian Esotericism 112
Christian faith 3, 8, 9, 24, 25, 32, 37, 52, 70, 120, 123, 124, 126
Christian heresy 12
Chrysochir 92
Church Fathers 16, 24, 26, 27, 28, 33, 41, 50, 53, 54, 73, 124, 125
cipher 57
Classical Paganism 34, 67
Clement 7, 27, 35, 45, 46, 48, 57, 59, 62, 63, 64, 71, 121
codex 30, 62, 84, 128
Consolamentum 99, 100
Constantine of Mananali 91
Constantinople 25, 37, 95, 96
Conze, Edward 116, 134
Coptic 29, 30, 31, 84, 89, 104, 127
Coptic Museum 31
Cosmas 92
cosmology 17, 38, 76, 78, 80, 125
Council of Nicaea 37
Council of Tours 95
Countess of Caithness 109
Count of Toulouse 100
Creator 29, 60, 76
Crowley, Aleister 111, 132

crucifixion 61, 82
Crusade 101
Cyprus 62

D

Demiurge 41, 44, 60, 63, 66, 79
demons 55, 97
deuterocanonical 21
Diaspora 17, 22, 67
Dick, Philip K. 115
Diocletian 67, 83
djinn 31
doctrines 6, 18, 26, 27, 41, 52, 53,
    54, 57, 59, 60, 61, 77, 78, 80,
    81, 82, 84, 87, 91, 92, 94, 96,
    106, 114, 122
Doinel, Jules 109, 110, 135
dream-bringers 55
Dualism 22, 95
Durrell, Lawrence 114, 136

E

Earth 41, 74, 85
Ecclesia Gnostica 111, 130
Ecclesia Gnostica Catholica 111
Ecclesiastical Councils 25
Edessa 75, 77
Edington 102
Edward Conze 116
Église Catholique Gnostique 110
Église Gnostique Universelle 110, 111
Egypt 15, 16, 17, 30, 31, 33, 36, 62, 69, 72, 83, 84
Ehrman, Bart D. 11, 120, 132
eighth day 45

Elchasai 74
elfin pedlars 1
Elkesaites 73, 74, 75, 80, 81
England 101, 102, 103, 111
Ennead 29
Ennoia 40
Ephesus 26
Epiphanius 28, 50, 54, 62, 65
Epistles 9, 19, 21, 25, 89, 121
Epton, Nina 102, 136
esotericism 34
Essenes 73
ethics 12
Eucharist 47, 64
Europe 15, 83, 93, 95, 103
evil 16, 31, 40, 41, 49, 50, 55, 58, 59,
    60, 61, 85, 86, 91, 115, 116
Exegetica 57

F

false doctrines 15
fellahin 31
first Adam 45
Five Commandments 88
Forster, E.M. 114, 134
Fournier, Jacques 101, 135
freemasons 106
Friedländer 15
Frost, Robert 113, 137

G

Galaad Centre 112
gems 33, 34
Gifts of the Spirit 23
Ginza 78
gnosis archive 111, 119, 131

Index

gnostic church 36, 109, 110, 119, 131
gnostic churches 6, 111
gnostic dualism 40
gnostic schools 8, 16, 26, 28, 33, 51, 53, 66, 119
gnostic theology 17, 105
'Goblin Market' 1
Gospel 7, 19, 30, 31, 35, 46, 47, 49, 50, 58, 60, 61, 62, 64, 65, 73, 81, 98, 99, 108, 121, 122
Gospel of John 19, 99
Gospel of Judas 31
Gospel of Mark 35, 121
Gospel of Mary 30
Gospel of Philip 46, 64, 73
Gospel of the Egyptians, 65
Gospel of Thomas 30, 49, 58, 64, 122
Gospel of Truth 62, 64, 65
Graeco-Roman 18, 23
Great King 74
Great Power 24
Green, Henry 22, 135
Guénon, René 110, 137
Guilhabert de Castres 98, 109

H

Haran Gawaita 78
Heavenly Twin 80
Helena 54
Hell 61
Heracleon 62
heresy 9, 12, 24, 26, 28, 34, 71, 91, 92, 95, 122, 125
Hermeticism 2

Hinduism 13
Hippolytus 27, 28, 41, 55, 57, 59, 62, 63, 64, 65, 66, 71, 73, 74
historians 5, 9, 15, 120
Hoeller, Stephan A. 111, 112, 119, 130, 131, 138
Holy Spirit 24, 37, 38, 62, 63, 74, 81, 94, 99, 100
Humpty Dumpty 8

I

Ialtabaoth 43
illuminating knowledge 23
initiation 73
invocation 48
iōta 48
Iranian dualism 16, 33, 40
Irenaeus 27, 28, 39, 40, 41, 43, 44, 50, 52, 54, 56, 57, 58, 59, 63, 65, 73, 95
Islam 77, 78, 87, 95
Italy 62, 93, 95

J

Jeffery, Peter 121, 137
Jesus 26, 37, 46, 48, 49, 51, 52, 57, 58, 59, 60, 62, 79, 81, 82, 86, 89, 94, 98, 112, 120, 122
Jewish 15, 16, 17, 18, 19, 21, 22, 23, 26, 33, 36, 56, 60, 61, 73, 77, 129
Jewish Diaspora 36
John 19, 24, 30, 41, 65, 79, 93, 94, 97, 99, 130
John the Baptist 79, 97
Judaism 15, 16, 18, 73

Gnosticism and Gnosis: An Introduction

Jung, C.G. 31, 117, 131, 133
Justin Martyr 26, 54

K

kabbalism 33
Karen King 12, 135
Kellis 84
khoikos 45, 46
King, Karen 12, 135
King of Light 79
Kingsford 109, 132
Kingsford, Anna 109, 132
Knights Templar 106

L

Lacarrière, Jacques 114, 135
Languedoc 95, 100, 112
Latin 30, 57, 84, 93
Lectorium Rosicrucianum 112
Léonce Fabre des Essarts 110
Lewis, H. Spencer 8, 111, 135
libraries 12
liturgical practises 64
Lombardy 95
love-philtres 55
Lower Egypt 17
Luckert, Karl 13, 135
Luke's Gospel 61
Lyons 27, 95, 99, 100

M

magic 55, 74
Mani 29, 75, 76, 77, 80, 81, 82, 83, 84, 85, 86, 87, 88, 89, 90, 91, 94, 95
Manichaeans 28, 76, 91, 94, 136

Manichees 75, 83, 87, 89
manuscripts 29, 30, 84, 87
Marcion 27, 28, 60, 61, 76
Marcionites 27, 76
Martinist Order 110
Mary 30, 37, 62, 63, 89, 97
Matter, 33
Matter, Jacques 33, 86
Mead, G.R.S. 34, 49, 107, 128, 135
Medinet Habou 30
Medinet Madi 84
Melville, Herman 113, 114, 135
Menander 56, 57
Mesopotamia 73
Miller, Henry 114, 135
Mithraism 16, 72
Montsegur 98, 101
More, Henry 9
Mosaic Law 54, 59, 93

N

Nablus 26
Nag Hammadi 31, 32, 35, 38, 46, 47, 49, 62, 64, 65, 66, 67, 69, 73, 83, 120, 122, 127, 128, 129, 130, 131
Nasoreans 75, 77
Nazarius 93
Neander, August 33, 132
Neoplatonist 17, 29, 67
New Testament 2, 19, 21, 23, 70, 89, 91, 94, 96, 120, 121, 128, 129
Nicene Creed 37, 38
Nicetas 96
Nock, A.D. 29

Index

North Africa, 17
Nous 44, 57
Nouvelle Église Gnostique 109

O

occultism 74
Oecumenical Councils 25
Old Testament 19, 21, 22, 60, 61, 71, 89, 96, 97
ōmega 48
Ophites 27, 51, 52, 113
Order of Bonshommes 102
Origen 28, 52, 71, 106
orthodoxy 18, 22, 24, 26, 29, 34, 37, 53, 70, 75, 105, 112, 121, 123
Oxyrhynchus 30

P

Pachomius 69
pagan 26, 28, 67, 108
Pagels, Elaine 120, 129, 134
Palestine 16, 17, 18, 36, 77
Panarion 28, 50, 54
Papus 110
Paraclete 81, 89
Paraphrase of Seth 66
Paterines 102
patriarchs 21
Paulicians 90, 91, 94
Pauline Epistles 19, 25
Perfecti 98, 101
Persian 82, 83
Peter 24, 30, 60, 91, 96, 121
Peter of Vaux-Sernai 96
Pétrement 16, 129

Petri, Catharose de 112, 113, 133
philosophical literature 22
philosophy 5, 6, 26, 34, 62, 71, 106, 119, 123
Pistis Sophia 30, 48, 49, 50, 128
Platonic dualism 40
Pleroma 39, 40, 41, 46, 51, 52, 58, 63
Plotinus 29, 40, 125
pneumatikos 45, 46
Pontus 60
Primal Man 85
prophets 7, 38, 79, 92, 93
Pseudepigrapha 21
psykhikos 45, 46
Ptolemaic Egypt 15
purification 73
Pythagorean 62

Q

quasi-masonic 109

R

realm of light 78
Red Book 117, 118
Reformed Churches 21
reincarnation 58, 59, 113
Reitzenstein 16
religious Orders 100
revealer 12, 13
Revelation of St. John 19
Richard, Duc de Palatine 111
ritual bathing 73
ritual practice 12
Roman Catholicism 9
Roman Empire 5, 8, 13, 25, 36, 66,

67, 72, 82, 90, 104, 105
Romantic Era 34
Rome 9, 26, 36, 55, 60, 62, 72, 73, 74, 83, 110
Rossetti, Christina 1, 133
Rudolph, Kurt 31, 39, 40, 54, 80, 105, 130, 136

S

Sacconi, Rainier 93, 95, 137
Sadducees 19
Salamis 28
Salmon, George 9, 10, 134
salvation 12, 37, 39, 46, 53, 55, 56, 58, 71, 78, 80, 85, 86, 87, 88, 98, 99, 100, 113, 123
Samaria 26
Samaritans 19, 24
Satan 93
Saturnilians 27
Saturnilus 56
scriptures 7, 18, 19, 32, 61, 69, 91, 122
second Adam 45
sects 9, 10, 15, 27, 32, 73, 80, 95, 107
Seleucia-Ctesiphon 80
Septuagint 18
Serbia 94
Sergius 91
Seth 65, 66
Sethian 65, 66
Seven Sermons to the Dead 117
Shapur I 82
Sige 44
Silk Road 82, 84, 90

Silvanus 91
Simon 23, 24, 48, 54, 55, 56, 58
Simon Magus 54
Sin 58
Sinope 60
Smith, Morton 10, 35, 121, 122, 131, 136
Solomon 22
Sophia 30, 41, 42, 44, 45, 48, 49, 50, 62, 128
soul 16, 45, 46, 52, 53, 59, 64, 78, 79, 86, 89, 99, 106
sparks of light 46
spirit-endowed 45
Spiritual Mysteries 107
St. Paul 8, 23, 91, 92
Sufism 110
Synoptic Gospels 19, 121

T

tarmidi 78
Tau Jean II 110
Tau Synesius 110
Tau Valentin II 109
ten powers 63
Tertullian 27, 28, 60, 65, 71
The Canonical Prayer Book 78
the Elect 86, 87, 88
The Gnostic Society 111
the Lord 7, 38, 46, 76, 94
the Mother 63
Theodosius 67
Theodotus 45, 47, 64
theologian 9, 27, 28, 75, 76, 83
Theosophical Society 107, 109
third Adam 45

Index

three powers 42
Three Seals 88
Three Steles of Seth 65
three types 45, 46, 64
Tigris 80
Timothy 8, 23, 61
Titus 61
Torah 18, 19
Toulouse 96, 98
transcendent 11, 12, 13, 14, 39, 40, 41, 42, 46
transcendent God 14, 39, 40, 41, 42, 46
treasuries 51
Treasury of the Light 49
Tree of Knowledge 81
Trinity 9, 93
Tripartite Tractate 64
Turkey 60
twelve powers 63
Tychicus 92

V

Valentinians 27, 39, 45, 50, 65, 66
Valentinus 27, 28, 39, 43, 62, 63, 64, 75, 109
Van Rijckenborgh, Jan 112, 135

W

Walter Map 102
Western Hermetic Tradition 2
William Blake 113
Williams, Michael 13, 54, 84, 130, 136
Wilson, Eric 70, 115, 116, 127, 128, 131, 134

Wisdom 22, 63, 111
wives 59

Y

Yamauchi 16, 130
Yeats, W.B. 113
Young Gnostic Brotherhood 112

Z

Zoroastrianism 16, 87